The Dyslexia Handbook 2009/10

Edited by **Dr Nicola Brunswick**
Managing Editor **Rachel Lawson**

Published by

The British Dyslexia Association
Unit 8 Bracknell Beeches, Old Bracknell Lane, Bracknell, RG12 7BW

Helpline: 0845 251 9002
Administration: 0845 251 9003
Website: www.bdadyslexia.org.uk
Front cover designer Jon Adams

9 781872 653501 >

ISBN 978-1-872653-50-1
£10.00 (inc. P&P)

British Dyslex!a
Association

The British Dyslexia Association

The British Dyslexia Association aims to ensure that there is a way forward for every dyslexic person so that he or she receives appropriate teaching, help and support, and is given an equal opportunity to achieve his or her potential.

The Dyslexia Handbook 2009/10

A compendium of articles and resources for dyslexic people, their families and teachers. The Dyslexia Handbook is substantially updated and revised each edition.

Edited by **Dr Nicola Brunswick**
Managing Editor **Rachel Lawson**

Published by
The British Dyslexia Association

Editorial Note

The views expressed in this book are those of the individual contributors, and do not necessarily represent the policy of the British Dyslexia Association.

The BDA does not endorse the advertisements included in this publication.

Whilst every effort has been made to ensure the accuracy of information given in this handbook, the BDA cannot accept responsibility for the consequences of any errors or omissions in that information.

In certain articles the masculine pronoun is used purely for the sake of convenience.

British Dyslexia Association

The Dyslexia Handbook 2009/10

1. Great Britain. Education
2. Title 11. Dr Nicola Brunswick
3. ISBN 978-1-872653-50-1

Published in Great Britain 2009 Copyright (c) British Dyslexia Association 2009

Printed by Bishops Printers Limited Portsmouth Hampshire
            www.bishops.co.uk

Advertising sales by Space Marketing
Tel: 01892 677740
Fax: 01892 677743
Email: brians@spacemarketing.co.uk

British Dyslexia Association
Unit 8, Bracknell Beeches, Old Bracknell Lane, Bracknell RG12 7BW
Helpline: 0845 251 9002
Administration: 0845 251 9003
Fax: 0845 251 9005

www.bdadyslexia.org.uk

BDA is a company limited by guarantee, registered in England No. 1830587
Registered Charity No. 289243

Contents

Strategies for success

Legislation

Biological factors in dyslexia

Reports from the dyslexia organisations

Recently published books on dyslexia

Editor's introduction:

Recent developments in dyslexia

Nicola Brunswick

The last few years have seen tremendous advances in the recognition of dyslexia and the support of dyslexic readers. Each development takes us a step closer to realising the BDA's goal of creating 'a dyslexia-friendly society so that all dyslexic people have the opportunity to achieve their full potential'.

This year's handbook reflects the most important of these developments, highlighting examples of good practice, governmental and educational initiatives relating to dyslexia, and cutting-edge research. The chapters vary in their focus – from children and young people in school, college and university to adults in the workplace; from identifying and managing dyslexic readers' difficulties to applauding their strengths; from looking back over recent achievements to looking forward with renewed optimism that the identification and support of dyslexia are increasingly being placed at the forefront of educational training, policy and practice.

These developments have occurred against the backdrop of the Secretary of State for Children, Schools and Families' announcement in December 2007 that:

> *"We need to be better at identifying pupils with dyslexia and then supporting them. Dyslexia is a particular need that requires particular attention... I want all schools to look closely at the support they offer for dyslexia, check that they are giving the most appropriate support available, and try to identify dyslexia where it may occur."*

One way in which pupils with dyslexia are to be supported is through the four year Inclusion Development Programme (IDP) which was launched by the Department of Children, Schools and Families (DCSF) in 2007. This aims to provide children who have special educational needs and disabilities with the benefit of mainstream schooling. A programme of continuing professional development aims to broaden teachers' knowledge of special educational needs, and increase their confidence in identifying and meeting the needs of these children.

Each year the IDP will focus on different special educational needs. In 2008, the focus was on dyslexia and speech, language and communication needs (SLCN). In particular, the programme aimed to bring about:

1. the earliest possible identification of dyslexia/SLCN, so appropriate support can be put in place at the first opportunity
2. an inclusive and supportive environment in which children with dyslexia/SLCN can learn
3. the raising of expectations and achievement by equipping teachers with the skills they need to support the specific needs of dyslexic/SLCN children in their classrooms, and
4. greater cooperation between local authorities and social services in supporting children with dyslexia/SLCN.

The section of this handbook on **Specialist dyslexia teaching** includes several chapters describing changes in dyslexia identification and support in primary and secondary schools, in the training of specialist dyslexia teachers, and in the promotion of a whole-school, dyslexia friendly ethos through Local Authority initiatives and the BDA Quality Mark.

The aims of the IDP are mirrored by the aims of the 'No to Failure' project – a collaboration between the BDA,

Xtraordinary People, Dyslexia Action and Patoss (funded by the DCSF) – which sought to measure the effectiveness of specialist teacher training in identifying and supporting children with dyslexia. It also sought to increase awareness of the needs of these children, to enhance inclusive practice within schools, and to raise expectations of what can be achieved by dyslexic children when specialist support is in place. The final report from 'No to Failure' was published in 2009, and Dr Chris Singleton and Rosie Wood have written about the aims and findings of the project in the **Special reports** section of this handbook.

The findings of 'No to Failure' have been considered by Sir Jim Rose who was asked by the DCSF to evaluate current provision for pupils with dyslexia, dyspraxia and dyscalculia, and to make recommendations on how the identification, teaching, and educational outcomes of these pupils might be improved. Professor Robert Burden (a member of Sir Jim's Expert Advisory Group) has summarised the main themes of the review for us.

Reliable information regarding specialist support and educational outcomes for dyslexic children across the country needs to be available not only to government advisors but also to parents and campaigners. To this end, July 2008 saw MP Sharon Hodgson's Special Educational Needs (Information) Bill pass successfully through parliament. Under this Bill, information on services that Local Authorities provide for children with dyslexia/SEN will be collected and published annually. This information will highlight best practice – identifying which authorities are providing the best support to their dyslexic/SEN pupils – and will help all children who require specific, additional educational support. Sharon has summarised her Bill, describing how and why it came into being, in the **Legislation** section.

Of course, not all dyslexic/SEN children are adequately supported in school. Parents whose concerns about their child's education have not been adequately addressed by the school may be forced to appeal to the Special Education Needs and Disability Tribunal. The structure of this tribunal changed in November 2008 when it ceased to exist as a single body, becoming instead a two tier tribunal. The first tier hears appeals against Local Authorities, and the second tier hears appeals against decisions made by the first tier tribunal. Full details of these changes, and the effects that they will have on the tribunal process, are presented by Lindy Springett.

The section entitled **Strategies for success** explores ways in which dyslexic children and adults can be helped to achieve their potential. Chapters in this section consider simple steps that parents can take to encourage their children's reading and spelling skills, and the use of multimedia presentations (MP3s, podcasts, animations, video recordings on YouTube) to support the teaching and learning of dyslexic students of all ages. This section ends with a look at the link between dyslexia and sporting preferences.

Although much of what we know about dyslexia has come from noting difficulties associated with reading, spelling, remembering and learning, the last decade or so has seen a dramatic increase in our knowledge and understanding of the genetic and biological bases of dyslexia. Our knowledge of which genes are involved in dyslexia has increased as a result of studies looking at the genetic makeup of dyslexic individuals, identical twins, non-identical twins and entire families with a high incidence of dyslexia. For example, October 2008 saw the identification of gene KIAA0319 on chromosome 6, which is carried by around 15% of the population, and linked to poor performance on tests of reading ability. Our knowledge of how these genes change the structure and function of the dyslexic brain has also expanded as neuro-imaging techniques allow us to explore similarities and differences between dyslexic and non-dyslexic brains. These issues are explored in the section on **Biological factors in dyslexia**.

It would be inappropriate to produce a dyslexia handbook in which the sole focus is on things that dyslexic readers struggle to do. As we all know, dyslexic children and adults also have many talents. Some of these talents were recognised in March 2009 at the launch of **Dyslexic, Dynamic and Determined!** This is a joint initiative between the BDA, Dyslexia Scotland, and Cass Business School (City University, London) to encourage dyslexic would-be entrepreneurs by offering them business mentoring from successful dyslexic entrepreneurs. This scheme developed from research which showed that around 35% of entrepreneurs in the US and 19% in the UK are dyslexic; this contrasts with figures of 1% in the US and 3% in the UK amongst business managers who work for other people. The authors of this study suggest that this may reflect coping strategies that dyslexic readers have developed throughout their lives – e.g. the ability to think through problems in a creative way, to pursue their dreams in spite of the obstacles, to motivate others to share their vision, and to surround themselves with people whose skills compensate for their own difficulties. The link between dyslexia, creative thinking and vision is explored in the section on **Dyslexia, creativity and the arts**.

Following the death in December 2008 of Professor Tim Miles, a chapter is dedicated to consider the remarkable contribution that this former Vice-President and founder member of the BDA made to our knowledge and understanding of dyslexia. His achievements were myriad and remarkable: setting up and developing the Dyslexia Unit at Bangor University; helping to establish the BDA; publishing research with dyslexic children and adults across five decades; developing the Bangor Dyslexia Test; tireless campaigning for the rights and needs of dyslexic readers, and editing the journal *Dyslexia*. He had a passionate enthusiasm for his subject that is evident in his many books. This was also clear for all to see in his oral presentation, at the age of 85, at the BDA International Conference in Harrogate in 2008. I am grateful to Ann Cooke from Bangor University for writing a tribute to Tim in celebration of his life and achievements.

Finally, I would like to thank a few people for their assistance in preparing this handbook: Judi Stewart and Rachel Lawson at the BDA; Chris Singleton, my editorial predecessor, for sharing his tremendous wealth of experience and contacts; Lindy Springett, from the Dyslexia Association of Bexley, Bromley, Greenwich & Lewisham, for her good-humoured advice; Dee Smith for producing the illustrations that you'll see at the start of each section, and all the chapter authors who generously gave their time and energy to share their experiences and examples of good practice.

Nicola Brunswick is Senior Lecturer in Psychology at Middlesex University, and a Trustee of the BDA

A new definition of dyslexia

Nicola Brunswick

There is no single, universally-accepted, definition of dyslexia. If you visit the websites of half a dozen dyslexia organisations, or read their literature, you will see half a dozen definitions describing dyslexia's symptoms, hinting at its possible cause, and listing other developmental difficulties that may co-occur with it.

A new definition of dyslexia has been produced in 2009 in Sir Jim Rose's 'Report on Identifying and Teaching Children and Young People with Dyslexia and Literacy Difficulties'. In preparing this report, Sir Jim and his Expert Advisory Group considered a vast array of evidence, and the BDA would like to thank everyone who contributed to this review, and acknowledge its enormous achievement in categorically establishing that dyslexia exists.

The definition of dyslexia adopted in the report is as follows[1]:

- "Dyslexia is a learning difficulty that primarily affects the skills involved in accurate and fluent word reading and spelling.
- Characteristic features of dyslexia are difficulties in phonological awareness, verbal memory and verbal processing speed.
- Dyslexia occurs across the range of intellectual abilities.
- It is best thought of as a continuum, not a distinct category, and there are no clear cut-off points.
- Co-occurring difficulties may be seen in aspects of language, motor co-ordination, mental calculation,

1 See Robert Burden's chapter in this handbook for a summary of the Rose review's findings; Robert was a member of the Expert Advisory Group

concentration and personal organisation, but these are not, by themselves, markers of dyslexia.

■ A good indication of the severity and persistence of dyslexic difficulties can be gained by examining how the individual responds or has responded to well founded intervention"

In addition to these characteristics, the BDA acknowledges the visual processing difficulties that some individuals with dyslexia can experience, and points out that dyslexic readers can show a combination of abilities and difficulties that affect the learning process. Some also have strengths in other areas, such as design, problem solving, creative skills, interactive skills and oral skills.

What does all this actually mean? Specifically:

■ Dyslexia manifests itself most clearly as a difficulty with learning to read and spell accurately and effortlessly.

■ Most dyslexic readers will also have difficulties with identifying and manipulating the sounds of language (e.g. recognising rhyming words or repeating made up non-words such as 'flimp'), holding verbal information in memory (e.g. remembering telephone numbers or people's names), and processing verbal information quickly and accurately (e.g. naming objects or colours).

■ Dyslexia can occur in people of below average intelligence, average intelligence, and above average intelligence.

■ Dyslexic readers differ in the severity of their reading difficulties just as non-dyslexic readers differ in their reading abilities, so there is no clear cut-off line between someone who is dyslexic and someone who is not dyslexic but simply a poor reader.

■ There are also signs of other developmental problems such as difficulties with acquiring spoken language (specific language impairment); poor motor skills and coordination (dyspraxia); difficulty with counting and with mental arithmetic (dyscalculia); poor concentration, inattention and hyperactivity (ADHD). Although these difficulties can occur alongside dyslexia, they are not in themselves signs of dyslexia.

■ For some dyslexic readers, a period of targeted support (in small-groups, preferably phonics-based and multi-sensory) can help them to make significant gains in their reading and spelling. Individuals with severe dyslexic difficulties will require more long-term, one-to-one support. For a small number, progress may be very slow and they may still never 'catch up' with their peers.

Dyslexic individuals can also experience difficulties with visual processing (including visual stress, visual tracking problems, binocular vision dysfunction, and difficulty with visuo-motor perception). They can experience letter and number reversals/mis-sequencing, lose their place when reading, see 'moving' letters when looking at the page, experience symptoms of fatigue with close work, show difficulties with visual word recall, and experience copying difficulties. However, their strengths can be many and varied; these can include artistic/design skills, verbal/visual creativity, and an original way of visualising/solving problems.

Should this new definition be adopted by the BDA? Before answering this question, it might be useful to consider the nature of a definition, and the uses to which we might put a definition of dyslexia.

A dictionary definition is a statement that expresses the meaning of a word, i.e. it briefly summarises the essential nature of something. By looking up the definition of a word, we can be sure that we all share the same understanding of what a word means. This is important.

It is also important to say that a definition is not the same as a description. Anyone who is familiar with dyslexia will appreciate that the definition adopted by the Rose review briefly summarises the key aspects of dyslexia. However, they will also be aware that it fails to encapsulate many of the daily problems of dyslexia. These might include confusing left and right, having difficulty learning a foreign language, being unsure if the bus that's approaching is the one that should be caught, producing written work that fails to reflect the individual's true ability, and poor time management. Common consequences of these difficulties are frustration and lack of confidence.

In considering the uses to which a definition might be put, we should note that the definition used in the Rose review is intended to be a starting point from which to evaluate educational provision and outcomes for children with dyslexia. As such, it is a working definition. It is not an operational definition of the kind that might be used by educational psychologists or specialist dyslexia teachers to diagnose dyslexia; by researchers to test a scientific theory of dyslexia; or by lawyers to advocate for the provision of financial or educational support to dyslexic students. Teachers, psychologists, researchers and lawyers have their own definitions of dyslexia that emphasise different aspects of its manifestation, but this does not detract from the validity of the Rose definition.

This notion was highlighted by Elaine Miles in her 1995 article 'Can there be a single definition of dyslexia?' when she suggested that:

"Dyslexia is not the sort of concept that can be summed up in a single formula; for different purposes different facets of dyslexia need to be mentioned." (p. 37)

This definition is not intended to replace others that are currently being used by professionals in their identification of dyslexia but it can sit alongside them, summarising the essential nature of dyslexia. It can be used by parents, teachers, journalists and the lay public so that they are all able to share a common understanding of what dyslexia is and, at the simplest level, how it manifests itself.

However, it's worth bearing in mind that whichever definition we use, we must note that the combination of symptoms will vary from person to person, from age to age, and from one situation to another. No single definition will fully encompass all the possible patterns of signs and symptoms that we might see in dyslexic children and adults in the real world. We are cautioned that:

"When we devise definitions in our field of research, we should not be too concerned about finding the one and only true definition. That may not even exist. We should instead be trying to devise the definition that best suits our purposes. That does exist." (Tønnessen, 1997, p. 85)

The definition that best suits the purposes of the Rose Review Expert Advisory Group is given at the start of this piece. The BDA also intends to adopt this definition, albeit with the addition of the paragraph on visual processing and possible dyslexic strengths given above. Other definitions are also available.

References

Miles, E. (1995). Can there be a single definition of dyslexia? *Dyslexia*, 1, 37-45.

Rose, J. (2009). *Identifying and Teaching Children and Young People with Dyslexia and Literacy Difficulties. Final report.* London: Department for Children, Schools and Families. Available at: http://www.dcsf.gov.uk/jimroseanddyslexia/

Tønnessen, F.E. (1997). How can we best define 'dyslexia'? *Dyslexia*, 3, 78-92.

A celebration of the life of Professor Tim Miles (1923 – 2008)

Ann Cooke

Tim Miles' interest in dyslexia was kindled at the very start of his academic career and he became a pioneer figure in the field. In his last book, *Fifty Years in Dyslexia Research* (2006), he says

> *"I have always taken the view that academic psychologists should not lose touch with what is sometimes called the 'real world'." (p29).*

In this account of his life and work I will try to provide a glimpse of that principle in action, the variety of his interests in dyslexia, and convey something of what made him and his work so special.

Family background and education

Tim and his older sister were taught at home by their mother until they were old enough to go away to prep school. She had a degree in Philosophy which must have stimulated his interest in ideas and discussion. She was also a fine pianist so he was introduced early to music, a love of which lasted throughout his life. Secondary education was at Winchester College and he went on to Oxford to take a degree in Greats. There he also developed his talents as a tennis player, captaining the University team and later, playing at Wimbledon. This too remained a life-long interest.

During the war he joined the army but his sense of morality and philosophical enquiry led him to a courageous decision: he applied for discharge as a conscientious objector. He had to defend his position at high levels but eventually his case was accepted and he returned to Oxford. The brush with authority perhaps gave him a personal insight into what it was like to be an 'outsider'. He certainly brought tremendous qualities of empathy to the children, parents, and adult dyslexics who came to him for help. People often went away feeling that a window had opened. Many of them wrote, sometimes years later, telling him that he had helped them change their lives.

The years at Oxford culminated in a change of direction which was to be crucial as he embarked on another degree – in the newly established Department of Experimental Psychology.

The psychologist

In 1949 he was appointed to a post at Bangor. As a psychologist his help was enlisted at the local Child Guidance Clinic where he was asked, on his very first day, to help a child who could not learn to spell, followed by another a while later. This was a decisive event. He recognised that these children's difficulties had a constitutional cause and began working out a way to help them learn. One of his early papers, *Two cases of developmental aphasia*, and a book chapter, *A suggested method of treatment for specific dyslexia* gave accounts of this work. On the strength of the first, he was invited to join the committee of the new Word-Blind Centre in London, a project for research, assessment and teaching which ran from 1962-1970.

Tim was therefore in at the beginning of the movement to investigate dyslexia in the UK, and he developed his own style of research. Initially this was mainly through assessment work and observation of individual cases that came to him. He also continued work on a method for teaching. By the early 1960s worried parents were seeking him out in Bangor and he began to study the diversity of symptoms amongst children with problems of reading and spelling.

Developments at Bangor

In 1963 Tim was active in setting up a new Department of Psychology, and was appointed as its first Professor. His assessment work continued and the range of research work on dyslexia expanded as new colleagues and PhD students began to collaborate.

His observations and enquiries led him to argue that dyslexia should be seen as a syndrome – a condition identified by its symptoms – which could include factors that went far beyond reading difficulties. Tim argued that it was a mistake to see dyslexia solely as a 'reading difficulty', and to believe that when individuals could read, they were no longer dyslexic. Dyslexics he said, *could* learn to read; spelling was a greater problem. Other aspects of language could be affected too, such as verbal expression, organisation of ideas and written work. Even personal organisation and left/right decisions (sometimes called 'soft signs' of dyslexia) could be part of the dyslexia syndrome. Each dyslexic individual would therefore show a distinctive cluster of difficulties, with a different range of intensities.

British Dyslexia Association

In 1972, Tim was a founder member of the BDA. He became a leading figure in its development and served to the end as a

Vice-President. By this time he had heard, from scores of parents, of the frustrations of children who needed help, how little was available, and how they had to fight for it. Knowledge about dyslexia in the teaching profession was minimal and disbelief in dyslexia was widespread; it was a contentious matter and he acquired a new role as campaigner. He began to be invited to address parents' meetings, to speak at conferences, write letters and serve on committees. Living in the north west corner of Wales meant long journeys but he rarely turned down an invitation. His wife Elaine was often included in these invitations and she shared her own ideas, particularly about teaching.

Bangor Dyslexia Unit

During the 1960s the scope of Tim's assessment and teaching work broadened. But he knew that assessment on its own was not enough. It was a relief to children and their parents to know the cause of the difficulties, but it was help they needed. He gained the interest of a local independent school and of the chief Medical Officer of Health in Anglesey, and children began to come for teaching. Elaine, a trained teacher, and a few others with similar training, joined in the work. This expanded when the county of Gwynedd was created in 1974. Children were referred after assessment by the LEA Educational Psychologists. The numbers were still quite small but the question was how to organise the work, how to recruit and train suitable teachers.

It was Elaine's idea that a Unit might be set up for this purpose, and she took on the role of Director of Teaching. It was decided that most children would have an hour a week help from a teacher who would visit the school, so Elaine began to recruit and train a team that could meet the needs.

Training was mainly reading, observation and then on the job, with Elaine available on the phone as trainer and mentor. Tim's book *On Helping the Dyslexic Child* (1970) was the teaching handbook, followed by their joint book *Help for Dyslexic Children* (1978) which took the work to secondary school level. They were the Miles team.

Travels and contacts

By this time, they had begun to attend national and international conferences and made lecture tours in America, Australia and New Zealand. Leading researchers also visited them in Bangor and Unit teachers were invited to meet them: Sally Childs, Margaret Rawson, Helen Arkell, Kathleen Hickey, Jean Augur, Harry Chasty and many others. Bevé Hornsby (then Head of the Dyslexia Clinic at St Bartholomew's Hospital in London) spent a year in Bangor working for her Masters degree. She and Tim published a paper on the rationale for their approaches and the results.

Training courses

A full time Masters degree was set up in the mid-70s in collaboration with the Department of Education. This was an academic course, though it included some teaching study. By 1980, Elaine and Tim realised that the academic degree was not enough: with more acceptance and identification of the need for knowledgeable teachers there was a growing need for practical training. A part-time Masters degree, running at weekends, made this possible. It attracted teachers from all over the country and from abroad.

As the courses, and the Unit, grew they took on lives of their own, and Tim wisely left them to get on with the job. But he was always interested in what was going on, ready to listen to teachers' observations, to answer and to encourage by attending teachers' meetings. Elaine continued as the Unit director of teaching until 1985, and as director of the courses till the early 90s. She and Tim made sure that others were able to take over, and the work has gone on to the present day.

The Bangor Dyslexia Test

By the mid-70s Tim had accumulated reports from several hundred assessments. He decided to develop a test which would identify dyslexia in children and in older students. Looking for common factors, he identified frequently recurring symptoms which added up to a distinctive pattern. This, along with marked underachievement in reading and/or spelling, would add up to a diagnosis. The resulting test, published in 1982, included a simple phonological task, tests of working memory, a mental subtraction test and a test for knowledge of left and right. Tim had noticed so often that dyslexia seemed to run in families that he included such incidence as a 'positive' point. He aimed to make the test straightforward to give and to score so that teachers could use it. Careful observation was necessary as he believed that the way children carried out the tasks could be informative. His book *Dyslexia: The Pattern of Difficulties* (1993) describes how the test was developed and its research background.

Dyslexia in adults

Tim's work in assessment, and his contributions to the growing awareness about dyslexia, strengthened his belief that dyslexia did not 'go away' even when literacy hurdles were largely overcome. When demands and situations changed it could re-surface in other ways. He noted that there were students in his department who were probably dyslexic, and arranged for a tutor (Dorothy Gilroy) to give them help with essay writing. This was the beginning of a campaign to get recognition and help for dyslexic students. He and Dorothy published *Dyslexia at College* in 1986 (the first of its kind, now in its 3rd edition) and the Bangor example began to be followed elsewhere.

It was not just in students that dyslexia and its effects needed to be recognised, but in all adults. Tim insisted throughout that dyslexia involved a different balance of skills and that dyslexic individuals, given understanding and the right conditions for work, could achieve as much in life as their non-dyslexic peers.

Others were involved of course, the BDA, the Adult Dyslexia Organisation, SKILL (the National Bureau for Students with Disabilities) and finally, the policy makers who included it as a disability in the Disabled Persons legislation. Tim gave encouragement, help and advice, attended meetings, wrote letters and emails; again he became a campaigner.

Other aspects of dyslexia

Tim also investigated the way that dyslexic learners coped with two other symbol systems, mathematics and music, and the effects that dyslexia could cause in these areas. In mathematics, the question was whether to refer to these children as 'dyscalculic', and he commented that it was a matter of knowing 'when to lump and when to split', whether to keep to one concept or develop a second. He was inclined to retain children who had problems with both kinds of symbol system within the dyslexia group. Typically, he was not dogmatic on the point. He and Elaine edited two books on dyslexia and mathematics, with contributions from researchers, teachers and dyslexics themselves.

His interest in music led Tim to take a leading role in setting up the BDA Music Committee which negotiated with the Associated Board of the Royal Schools of Music examinations for special arrangements for dyslexic candidates. This brought two books on dyslexia and music jointly edited with John Westcombe.

Frequently, Tim heard accounts of the way that the extra efforts needed to cope with dyslexic difficulties could cause a level of stress that was itself disabling. With another psychologist, Ved Varma, he edited *Dyslexia and Stress* (2004), in which dyslexic young people and their parents gave accounts of the different ways in which dyslexia affected them: school and college work, battles for assessment and teaching, and attitudes of others at school and at work.

Retirement, honours and awards

Tim retired from his University post in 1987 and was granted the title Professor Emeritus. His work in dyslexia, and for dyslexic people, continued. It brought him wide recognition, many academic honours and awards, and in 2004, the OBE. In 1994 a Festschrift was published to mark his work; it included a chapter of his own! The T.R. Miles lectures, given annually to a public audience, started in 1996 and brought to Bangor leading UK and international authorities. The previous year he had become founding editor of the BDA journal *Dyslexia – An International Journal of Research and Practice*; true to his principles, he insisted that it should include papers on practical matters, such as teaching. One must remember also that his academic work was not restricted to dyslexia: he wrote on aspects of behavioural psychology, philosophy, and religious belief (his own beliefs had led him in 1960, with Elaine, to become a Quaker). His writing was eloquent, clear and without jargon, for he was essentially a communicator and a teacher. He has left a valuable account of his work in *Fifty Years in Dyslexia Research* (2007) which is a delight to read. Setting an example of how not to retire, he went on working to the end of his life.

Tim Miles was a very kind man, with a warm sense of humour and an amazing memory. He was greatly respected and admired, and those who knew him regarded him with much affection. Latterly he coped patiently with heart troubles and increasing loss of eyesight. Essentially an optimist, Tim said that if he wrote an autobiography it ought to be called 'Look Back in Happiness'. That is how he would wish to be remembered.

References

Miles, T.R. (1961). Two cases of developmental aphasia. *Journal of Child Psychology and Psychiatry*, 2, 48-70.

Miles, T.R. (1964). A suggested method of treatment for specific dyslexia. In A.W. Franklin (Ed.) *Word Blindness or Specific Developmental Dyslexia*. London: Pitman.

Miles, T.R. (1970). *On Helping the Dyslexic Child*. London: Methuen Educational

Miles, T.R. (1978). *Help for Dyslexic Children*. London: Methuen Educational

Miles, T.R. (1993). *Dyslexia: The Pattern of Difficulties* (2nd edition). London: Whurr.

Miles, T.R. (2006). *Fifty Years in Dyslexia Research*. Chichester: Wiley Blackwell

DuPré, E.A., Gilroy, D., and Miles, T.R. (2006). *Dyslexia at College*. (New edition) London: Routledge Falmer.

Hornsby, B. & Miles, T.R. (1980). The effects of a dyslexia-centred teaching programme, *British Journal of Educational Psychology*, 50, 236-42.

Miles, T.R. & Miles, E. (2004). *Dyslexia and Mathematics.* London: Routledge Falmer.

Miles, T.R. & Varma, V. (2004). *Dyslexia and Stress* (2nd edition). Chichester: John Wiley & Sons.

Miles, T.R. & Westcombe, J. (2008). *Music and Dyslexia: Opening New Doors* (New edition). Oxford: Wiley-Blackwell.

Ann Cooke is Director of the Masters modules on Dyslexia at the Bangor Dyslexia Unit. She was for some years Director of the Unit.

Special reports

dyslexia..
more
than
words.

DYSLEXIA
FACT-NOT-FICTION

80%	TRUANTS
70%	YOUNG OFFENDERS
50%	PRISON POPULATION
41%	UNEMPLOYED
25%	FUNCTIONALLY ILLITERATE
10%	GENERAL POPULATION
4%	SEVERE DYSLEXIC/HE STUDENTS

We offer the following services **Dyslexia Awareness** and Identification Btec Level 3 **Dyslexia Screening Software** Dyslexia Screening Dyslexia Assessment for Education Dyslexia Assessment for Employment Dyslexia Tuition Employment Retention Support Dyslexia Mentoring Dyslexia **Vocational Support** Workplace Technical Needs Assessment Consultancy for Policy & Legislation Funding and Grant AdviceHelpline and Online Support Dyslexia Awareness and Identification Btec Level 3 Our dyslexia training course is either 1 or 2 days and is accredited by BTEC at Level 3. The training is aimed to give the individual the skills to work and support **dyslexic adults.** It covers the history of dyslexia, identification teaching practice and working practice. The training has been undertaken by many national and regional organisations working in the public private and third sector organisations. The training can be delivered in a bespoke manner addressing all attendee's needs. Dyslexia Screening

adult-dyslexia-access [northwest]
4th Floor 3Tc Crosby Road North Liverpool L22 0NY
email: adainuk@aol.com website: www.dyslexia-help.org
helpline: **+44 (0)800 077 8763**

adult-dyslexia-access

helpline: **+44 (0)800 077 8763**

Fulneck School, Leeds

There is no barrier to success

Independent day & boarding school
Ages 3-18
Specialist Learning Support Unit
CReSTeD registered School
(Council for the Registration of Schools teaching Dyslexic Pupils)

At Fulneck School we aim to identify individual special needs and to provide teaching programmes and strategies to allow all students access to the curriculum at a level commensurate with their intellectual ability.

As a category DU registered School offering a Dyslexia Unit, Fulneck School offers specialist one-to-one tuition within the school as well as support for dyslexic students in all areas of the curriculum.

The pupils can take advantage of individual and small group tuition from experienced specialist teachers, multi-sensory teaching methods and continuity of teaching and support throughout their school career. Our pupils have access to specialist computer software in a dedicated unit to ensure a relaxed, safe and secure learning environment. In-class support is also provided if required.

Contact us today to find out how your child can benefit from a Fulneck School education:
+44 (0)113 257 0235 or
enquiries@fulneckschool.co.uk

Fulneck School
Pudsey, Leeds
England, LS28 8DS
www.fulneckschool.co.uk
Registered Charity

Identifying and teaching children and young people with dyslexia and literacy difficulties: The Rose review of dyslexia

Professor Robert Burden

In May 2008 the Secretary of State for Education invited Sir Jim Rose to review the situation within English schools with regard to the identification and treatment of dyslexia. A call for evidence was made within the media in July of that year and 863 responses were received. Most of these were from parents or carers of dyslexic children, but a substantial number were from teachers or researchers and from children and adults suffering from dyslexia.

A panel of experts was called together, mainly from the academic sector most involved in dyslexia research and evaluation, but also including representatives from teaching organisations and one centre for dyslexic children. A wide-ranging review of current literature was carried out, visits were made to a number of schools, and consultations were held with practitioners providing specific inputs for dyslexic children. The panel (two of whom were members of the BDA Accreditation Board) met on a regular basis over an eight month period to sift through the evidence and shape up the final report.

By the end of June 2009 a final report had been prepared and was ready for submission to the Secretary of State. It provided a summary of main findings and recommendations for action, together with comprehensive details of the evidence base upon which these were built. The issue of an appropriate definition is carefully considered in the report, and a new definition offered, derived from an evidence-based analysis of those that have gone before. However, no claim is made that this definition covers every issue or that it should necessarily be widely accepted. The issue of early and appropriate identification is also examined, as are the nature of services across the country supporting schools, children and their families, the role and training of specialist dyslexic teachers, evidence on proven ways of tackling reading difficulties, and the issue of co-occurring difficulties. As part of the original remit, specific attention is given to the positive outcomes of 'Every Child a Reader' and of the 'No to Failure' projects.

Perhaps the most important aspect of the Rose Report is its 19 recommendations, all of which have been accepted by the Secretary of State for Children Schools and Families. Specifically, the DCSF is now committed to providing extra funding for teachers to undertake appropriate accredited specialist training in teaching children with dyslexia, as well as supporting initiatives for strengthening coverage of SEN, including dyslexia, on initial teacher education courses.

The Rose Report is the first of its kind ever carried out on behalf of a Government department anywhere in the world. It is bound to have a significant impact on the life opportunities of all those faced with dyslexic difficulties, particularly in the early years of schooling. It is essential reading for anyone connected in any way with children or adults with dyslexia, and it is hoped that it will serve as a shining beacon for dyslexic readers everywhere.

Robert Burden is Chair of the BDA Accreditation Board and a member of the Rose Expert Advisory Group

'No to Failure': the results of the intervention study

Chris Singleton

'No to Failure' is the single largest empirical study of intervention for dyslexia ever carried out in the UK. For this reason alone, the results of the project are bound to be of enormous importance. But, as Rosie Wood explains in her chapter, 'No to Failure' has been much more than a conventional research project. It has also included an extensive programme of teacher-training and awareness raising, as well as close collaboration with schools and local authorities, activities that have all been very successful in their own right. The aim of this chapter is to outline the main findings of the intervention study, which have been published in full in the final report of the project, available on the Dyslexia-SpLD Trust website (www.thedyslexia-spldtrust.org.uk).

My role in the project was independent evaluator, responsible for analysing the data, evaluating the findings and writing up the results. I did not play any part in designing the project, in selecting the schools or tests, or in delivering the intervention. However, I did not have to carry out my job completely alone, because I had support from the 'No to Failure' Steering Committee, from Rosie Wood, SpLD specialist advisor to the project, and from project manager Sandy Fitzgerald. Dr Jo Horne, lecturer in psychological statistics at the University of Hull, also assisted in the data analysis, and I received useful critical feedback on earlier drafts of the results from members of the Dyslexia Expert Advisory Group; this was set up by Sir Jim Rose to assist him in the preparation of a review on educational provision for dyslexic children, which was requested by Ed Balls, the Secretary of State for Children, Schools and Families. An additional task that I undertook was to carry out a detailed review of international research on specialist teaching for dyslexia (Singleton, 2009).

The design of the project

'No to Failure' was not originally conceived as an empirical research study. However, after the project had commenced, it became clear that in order to provide robust evidence that would support the call for a specialist dyslexia/SpLD teacher in every school, a much more scientific approach would be necessary. By the time this was appreciated, the children who would receive intervention had already been identified by a screening process and much of the specialist teaching had already commenced. Rosie Wood and I contributed a chapter to the 2008-09 edition of the BDA Dyslexia Handbook that outlined the findings of the screening phase of the 'No to Failure' project (Singleton and Wood, 2008), so I will not be covering those results here, although there are some important issues connected with screening that I will raise in the concluding section.

Of a total of 1,164 children from years 3 and 7 who had been screened in the 19 participating schools, 243 children (21% of the original sample) were found to be at risk of dyslexia/SpLD. However, because available funds were sufficient to provide specialist teaching for less than half the pupils found to be at risk, teachers naturally chose for tuition those children who they thought were most in need of help. Thus, 108 of the at-risk pupils commenced weekly 1:1 or paired instruction from a specialist teacher, using well-established phonologically-based systematic multisensory teaching techniques. It was at this point that the project had to be turned into an empirical research study capable of yielding quantitative data that could be analysed statistically. Although this transformation was successfully accomplished, inevitably there were methodological limitations. Specialist teaching had already started, so it was too late to assign at-risk children at random to an 'intervention group' and a 'control group', which is the 'gold standard' method for research of this type. It was also too late to reconsider the tests that were being used, which had been selected for the purposes of screening and to give teachers diagnostic information about the pupils that would help in formulating teaching strategies, rather than for the purpose of evaluating the effects of an intervention. Consequently, the only realistic option was to assign the remaining 135 at-risk children who were not already receiving specialist tuition to a 'comparison group', to stick with the tests already in use – however far from ideal – and see what happened. But, as can be seen from the results reported in this chapter, the children in the comparison group, on average, had less severe difficulties than the children in the intervention group.

Figure 1 shows the design of the intervention. The pupils in the intervention group each received specialist tuition over 20 weeks. However, although the target was 20 hours of

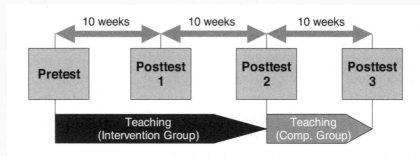

Figure 1. The design of the 'No to Failure' intervention study

specialist teaching at one hour per week, for various practical reasons this target was not always achieved; in fact, the average amount of instruction given was 16.8 hours. All the pupils (those in the comparison group as well as those in the intervention group) were tested at the outset of the study (pre-test), again after 10 weeks (post-test 1), and also at the end of the 20 week teaching period (post-test 2). Subsequently, DCSF provided additional funds to enable pupils in the comparison group to be offered 10 weeks of specialist tuition, after which these pupils were administered a further post-test (post-test 3), although there were insufficient resources to re-test the pupils in the intervention group again at this point.

Results

Figure 2 shows the impact of the intervention on phonic decoding fluency, as measured by the Phonemic Decoding Efficiency test of the Test of Word Reading Efficiency (TOWRE)[2]. It can be seen that although the intervention group started some way behind the comparison group, by the end of the 20 week tuition period, the intervention group had more-or-less caught up with the comparison group. This gain was statistically significant for the Year 3 pupils, for whom phonic decoding ability was raised to within the normal range. Unfortunately, however, this effect was not found for the Year 7 pupils, whose difficulties were more severe than those of the younger children, and who consequently proved a more challenging proposition.

When the pupils in the comparison group were given specialist dyslexia/SpLD tuition, a strong impact on phonic decoding skills was found (see Figure 2). Since the difficulties exhibited by the children in this group were less severe than those shown by the intervention group, we might in any event have

2 To save space in this chapter I have shown results for Years 3 and 7 combined, but the final report of the study shows a full breakdown of results for Years 3 and 7 separately.

expected rather better rates of gain in the comparison group when provided with additional tuition. On the other hand, the comparison group pupils only received 10 weeks' specialist tuition, compared with 20 weeks given to the intervention group, so in this context, the accelerated gains made by the comparison group pupils demonstrate the benefits that these pupils derived from the teaching programme.

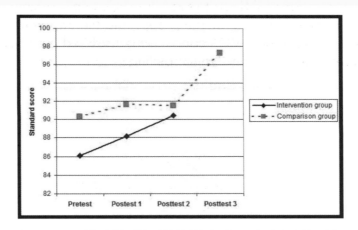

Figure 2. Impact of the intervention on phonic decoding fluency (combined data for Years 3 and Year 7).

Figure 3 shows the results for spelling, based on assessment using the Vernon Spelling test. Both Year 3 and Year 7 intervention groups showed statistically significant gains in spelling compared with the comparison group. For Year 3 the average gain in spelling was over 10 standard score points, and for Year 7 it was 6 standard score points. But despite these encouraging gains, spelling remained well below the normal range, demonstrating that longer intervention is necessary to 'normalise' the spelling of dyslexic children. Again, when the pupils in the comparison group were given specialist tuition, significant impact on spelling development was seen.

Analysis of data on the children's progress in reading, obtained from the New Macmillan Reading Assessment (NMRA), was restricted because this test gives reading ages rather than standard scores. Year 3 pupils in the intervention group made an average of 7–8 months gain in reading accuracy and comprehension, while Year 7 pupils made smaller gains of about 3–5 months. Unfortunately, however, because of lack of staff and resources it was not possible to give this test to the comparison group, and therefore the statistical results for NMRA cannot be considered as robust as those reported for phonics and spelling.

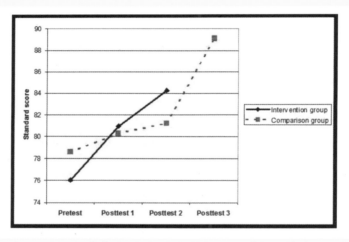

Figure 3. Impact of the intervention on spelling ability (combined data for Year 3 and Year 7).

Discussion

The results of the 'No to Failure' project not only confirm that specialist dyslexia/SpLD teaching works (which many of those working in this field have known for a very long time), but also indicate that the provision of a relatively brief intervention can make a marked difference to the literacy skills of many dyslexic pupils. On a range of different literacy measures, 51% of Year 3 pupils and 44% of Year 7 pupils made 'good' progress in response to specialist teaching – i.e. they gained at least 5 standard score points or 5 months in reading age on the tests during the intervention; a further 25% made some progress. Of course, 16 hours of specialist instruction is not sufficient to 'normalise' the literacy skills of these pupils – they will need continuing support for some time to come – but it is a significant start. These results also compare favourably with other phonologically-based intervention studies for pupils with dyslexia carried out in the UK and USA, especially when the relative brevity of the 'No to Failure' intervention is taken into account (for a review of other research studies see Singleton, 2009). Many teachers noted the remarkable changes in the pupils who had received specialist teaching, commenting on their improved self-confidence, willingness to 'have a go', and greater independence as learners.

It is apparent, however, that progress was more marked for Year 3 pupils than for Year 7 pupils, especially in phonic skills. This confirms the common finding that older dyslexic pupils are more difficult to remediate than younger ones. Providing effective intervention for older dyslexic pupils – who typically have more severe problems – in an average of only 16 hours is extremely difficult and it is unsurprising that few made dramatic leaps forward. Simply preventing such pupils slipping backwards relative to their more literate peers is not an easy task; to reverse this trend is a considerable feat. In spite of these obstacles, however, a substantial proportion of the Year 7 pupils made encouraging progress. The intervention in the study was time-limited, but given the published evidence available from longer intervention studies, it is reasonable to suppose that the accelerated levels of progress would have continued if the specialist teaching had continued.

The method of screening adopted in the project was a pragmatic choice to suit the circumstances and is not put forward as necessarily an ideal or 'best' solution to identifying pupils with dyslexia/SpLD. But as a result of that screening, a considerable number of pupils were classified as being 'at-risk' who were not on the SEN register, and who therefore appear to have slipped through the SEN 'net', suggesting that screening can be a useful tool. However, the inevitable limitations of any screening process imply that some children in the study may have been misclassified as being at risk of dyslexia/SpLD when their literacy difficulties had other causes. It certainly cannot be assumed that all the at-risk children will have had appropriate learning opportunities at all stages of their education. But whether children's failure to make progress is due to inherent learning difficulties or to other factors, this highlights the importance of teachers noticing children who are falling behind and adjusting their teaching to help those children to catch up, regardless of whether or not the children concerned are considered to have special educational needs. The findings of the study also underline the need for schools to have good access to expertise and procedures for identifying all pupils falling behind, including those with SEN (amongst whom would be those with dyslexia/SpLD). Many of these at present appear to be slipping through the net, and are therefore making less progress than they might if they were to receive teaching tailored to their strengths and areas of difficulty. Part of that process must surely be the enhancement of the knowledge base and expertise of all teachers to notice when children are not making appropriate progress and to adjust their teaching accordingly. However, specialist dyslexia/SpLD teachers have a key role to play in training classroom teachers and teaching assistants, and in facilitating identification in the classroom, as well as in delivery and management of effective solutions for children identified with dyslexia/SpLD.

References

Singleton, C. (2009). *Intervention for Dyslexia: A review of published evidence on the impact of specialist dyslexia teaching.* Dyslexia-SpLD Trust (www.thedyslexia-spldtrust.org.uk).

Singleton, C. & Wood, R. (2008). No To Failure. In C. Singleton (Ed.) *The Dyslexia Handbook 2008/9.* Bracknell, Berks: British Dyslexia Association (pp. 22-29).

Dr Chris Singleton is senior lecturer in educational psychology at the University of Hull and research director of Lucid Research Ltd. He was independent evaluator of the 'No to Failure' project and a member of the DCSF Expert Advisory Group on Dyslexia that assisted Sir Jim Rose in preparing his report on the identification and teaching of dyslexic pupils. He is also associate editor of the *Journal of Research in Reading.*

'No to Failure': the bigger picture

Rosie Wood

The 'No to Failure' two year project, which began in February 2007, is now complete. An interim report was published in June 2008 and the final report is due for publication in May 2009.

Chris Singleton and I wrote an article for the 2008/9 BDA Dyslexia Handbook in which the results of the 'No to Failure' screening process in schools were discussed (Singleton and Wood, 2008). In his chapter of the current handbook, Chris Singleton discusses the intervention results from the specialist tuition which followed for pupils designated as 'at risk' of dyslexia/SpLD from that screening.

How did it all start?

The seeds which grew to become the 'No to Failure' project were sown in the early days of 2004 at the Helen Arkell Dyslexia Centre. Kate Griggs, the dyslexic mother of two dyslexic boys, came to the Centre for advice on assessments and help in getting the right support for her boys' education. Fired by the inequity of a situation in which she was able to fund the support to enable *her* boys to flourish and learn, but which was not necessarily available to families without the means to pay, Kate formed, and began to work under the banner of, Xtraordinary People (XP). Her aims were to raise:

- awareness of dyslexia and Specific Learning Difficulties (SpLD), and the need for all schools to provide the right support
- expectations for children with dyslexia – who can achieve if

they are recognised early, and given timely and appropriate intervention
- money for the essential teacher training in dyslexia so that schools have the necessary expertise in-house

First links with the Department for Education and Schools: DfES

The catalyst for the project was when XP joined forces with national dyslexia organisations – the British Dyslexia Association (BDA), Dyslexia Institute (soon to become Dyslexia Action) and the Professional Association for Teachers of Students with Specific Learning Difficulties (PATOSS) – so these organisations began to work together and to speak with 'one voice'. In 2007 the Department agreed to fund a project to be run by the group, and the 'No to Failure' project was born!

Project aims

'No to Failure' started with a firm focus on public relations and awareness raising, aiming to:

Communicate:

- why dyslexia/SpLD training is essential – for quality-first teaching in the classroom and to provide specialist teachers to work with pupils with more complex dyslexia/SpLD
- the links between pupils 'failing' and inadequate support for those with dyslexia/SpLD

Demonstrate:

- how to 'get it right' by developing exemplar 'Trailblazer' schools across the country

- existing good practice against the background of prevailing inconsistency of provision in schools

There is, of course, funding in the education system already to support Special Educational Needs (SEN). 'No to Failure' wanted to encourage schools to re-examine their existing budgets such as the School Development Grant, SEN and Personalised Learning budgets, and question whether they were getting the best value from these in terms of improving outcomes for pupils with SEN, and in gaining effective training and support in SEN. 'No to Failure' support was designed to link closely to the SEN Code of Practice, i.e. 'a focus on early identification and support by appropriately trained staff'.

'No to Failure' and Local Authorities

In 2007 talks were held with several Local Authorities (LAs) about participation. The project plan was to cover both a geographical and socio-economic mix. 'No to Failure' was fortunate that three very different LAs across inner city, suburban, rural and coastal settings – Southwark, Calderdale and Cornwall – agreed to participate. Each of the authorities had already made a solid commitment to inclusion, and was commendably flexible in fitting 'No to Failure' into existing plans and integrating it with other initiatives.

The result was that the heart of the project was a cluster of Trailblazer schools, both primary and secondary, in each Local Authority and, in Southwark, one pupil referral unit (PRU) and a school for pupils with social and emotional difficulties (SEBD).

'No to Failure' in action

The 'No to Failure' project aimed to 'skill up' schools to enable them to be more fully inclusive. To do this it offered each Trailblazer school a range of support including screening, specialist tuition and training:

- **Foundation training**: whole staff awareness and understanding of dyslexia/SpLD, along with a practical knowledge of effective classroom strategies. The premise behind this is simple: if *all* staff are skilled to this level, many pupils with milder difficulties will be well catered for within the normal classroom, and fewer pupils will actually need the support of a specialist

- **Specialist teacher training**: for some staff. This was designed to provide a resident specialist in each school (or in the case of very small schools, a 'shared' specialist) so that every pupil with more severe dyslexia/SpLD has immediate access to a specialist in school who can also offer professional support and guidance to pupils, colleagues and parents

- **Experience of screening, assessment, planning and delivery of individual learning programmes**: staff in each school were encouraged to work together with 'No to Failure' tutors in screening all pupils in years 3 and 7 (and all primary years in the PRU and SEBD school), and in liaising over tuition programmes

- **Resources:** to assist screening, assessment and support programmes. Resources have now been given to schools in the LAs for them to continue using to screen and support pupils. Many useful resources were copied from 'No to

Failure' tutors and used immediately with other pupils, augmenting the school resource base in classrooms

- **Specialist tuition for 'at risk' pupils** in year 3 and 7. 'No to Failure' dyslexia/SpLD specialists taught pupils for a maximum of 20 hours over two terms. 'No to Failure' specialists used their training and experience to design individual, tailored programmes for each pupil

- **'Master class' experience** for Teaching Assistants (TAs) 'shadowing' the specialist tuition. Where it was possible TAs joined the 'No to Failure' lessons and followed these with practice activities in the week, giving valuable feedback to be used in adapting the weekly programme

- **Feedback to each school**: screening and post-test results, and final reports on taught pupils. Full details were given to each school for use in planning and provision, and for dissemination to other professionals and parents

In practice each school had slightly different needs. A great strength of the NTF project was that it was flexible enough to adapt to these. 'One size does not fit all' is definitely true in the dyslexia/SpLD field; each school, like each pupil, has a unique profile and, whilst keeping the support based on firm but simple principles, 'No to Failure' was able to adapt to that profile.

Foundation Training input varied according to requirements. In some schools, the whole staff attended a three day programme covering literacy development, awareness and identification of dyslexia, and effective classroom strategies; in others the input was more focused, for instance subject-specific support in secondary school, or practical days for TAs followed by a summary presentation for teachers.

Specialist Training was based on the 'No to Failure' recommended pyramid of training (see Figure 1), offering training at levels two and three of the pyramid, i.e.

BDA – ATS level: Approved Teacher Status
BDA – AMBDA level: Approved Member of the BDA

Each Local Authority embraced a different specialist training model:

In **Calderdale**, starting in September 2009, 25 teachers from Calderdale have the opportunity to train on an AMBDA level course at Manchester Metropolitan University.

In **Cornwall**, teachers and TAs have trained on the ATS course at St Austell College. DCSF funding permitting, more will train on the blended e-learning ATS and AMBDA level courses run by Dyslexia Action (see Anne Sheddick's chapter in this handbook).

In **Southwark** there was a strong preference for setting up a training centre to ensure sustainability within the borough. 'No to Failure' funded the first cohort of teachers and teaching assistants in a training centre established in the new Lyndhurst Dyslexia Centre which received OCR approval in 2007/8.

In addition to the 'No to Failure' funded teachers, four further teachers from south-east London have been offered training through the generosity of Fairley House School, a specialist school for dyslexic pupils which runs an ATS level course.

Screening was designed with the original aims of the project

NTF Training Pyramid

Diploma
BDA AMBDA Accredited *

Certificate
BDA ATS Accredited **

Foundation training
For all teachers and teaching assistants to include Inclusion Development
Programme, letters and sounds / synthetic phonics training

Understand the acquisition of literacy skills
Understand barriers to learning
Recognise SpLDs in the classroom
Early intervention strategies and classroom support
Phonological awareness and building basic skills of literacy
Introduction to learning styles and developing independent learning
Awareness for teachers and LSAs
Contribute to a supportive environment
Be familiar with principles of effective teaching and learning
Understand the nature of communication difficulties, dyslexia and other SpLDs

*AMBDA Accredited

Training accredited as meeting requirements for Associate Membership of the British Dyslexia Association (BDA). These are Level 7 qualifications on the QCA framework.

**ATS Accredited

Training accredited as meeting requirements for Approved Teacher Status by the British Dyslexia Association. These are Level 5 qualifications on the QCA framework.

Figure 1

in mind, and therefore tests were chosen to be valuable both in identifying pupils 'at risk' of dyslexia/SpLD and in providing the 'No to Failure' specialists with as much information as possible on which to plan an individual programme of tuition. This was essential as there was not time to carry out full diagnostic assessments, and the aim was to maximise the value of a very short period of specialist input (an average of 16.8 hours per pupil).

Sign in Head-teacher's office in Calderdale – chiming with our own approach!

Problems and Solutions! Once the 'No to Failure' project was well under way, with screening and tuition having already started, the DCSF asked for the emphasis to be moved closer to a research project to produce statistics on screening for dyslexia, and to measure the value of specialist tuition against a comparison group. Inevitably there were methodological limitations, including the lack of a true control group and a less-than-ideal test battery, which compromised results. Pupils who had been identified as 'at risk' but who did not receive tuition immediately became the 'comparison group' who were offered tuition after the main tuition programme had finished; these were, inevitably, pupils with less severe problems as staff had naturally selected those with the more severe learning difficulties for immediate support.

However, despite these disadvantages, it *has* proved possible to produce useful figures showing the prevalence of dyslexia in both primary and secondary schools (at years 3 and 7), and the value of tuition from specialists (in literacy gains and confidence) over even a short period.

Specialist tuition was from trained specialists who use a toolkit of skills based on their training, this includes:

- a thorough understanding of the structure of language
- the theory of literacy learning
- deficits which may underlie literacy difficulties (including detailed knowledge of phonological deficits)
- synthetic phonics
- the full phonic structure

Their teaching programmes were initially developed from:

- the screening results
- further assessment in their first lesson
- information from the school

Based on this was a programme of 'analytic' teaching which continually 'fine tuned' tuition to the pupil's changing needs and developing skills. Tuition aimed to improve not only literacy but also organisation, concentration and learning so that each pupil was then able to access the curriculum, and become an independent learner. Each and every lesson was multi-sensory, structured, cumulative, and individually tailored not only to the pupil's needs but also to his or her interests, teaching metacognitive awareness (where the learner understands the nature of the task, his

SENCo and successful pupil in Southwark

own strengths and weaknesses and *what works* for him), and building self-confidence based on measurable steps to success.

Evaluation and Dissemination

Towards the end of the project, each Local Authority and all schools participated in a wide ranging evaluation exercise. Evaluation visits, questionnaires, a stakeholder day involving all three LAs and a road-show day in each area, all contributed to rich feedback at every level to add to the statistical analysis undertaken by Dr Chris Singleton and Dr Jo Horne of Hull University.

Staff in all three LAs, who were uniformly friendly and helpful throughout, were committed to the project and its aims of 'skilling up' schools in the interests of real inclusion for pupils 'at risk' of dyslexia/SpLD. The 'good fit' of 'No to Failure' with their existing plans and initiatives was evident. Commitment of senior staff in schools was clearly crucial to success, including planning workload to allow staff to participate. Teachers and TAs saw the training as valuable for their own continuing professional development and appreciated the progress made by the pupils. On the top of many teachers' 'wish lists' was a specialist in their school!

Parents described the positive effects of specialist teaching as they reported improvements at school and at home.

Teamwork in Cornwall: Headteacher, SENCo, pupil and 'No to Failure' specialist

Their children were keener to come to school, they were less frustrated, and showed increased confidence and self-esteem.

All were keen to continue the work of the project, and in all three LAs there are ongoing

Mum and 'star' pupil in Calderdale

plans. In Calderdale a new authority inclusion mark will include and build on the work done with dyslexia/SpLD. Cornwall is closely involved with the Inclusion Development Programme (IDP) and each school has a 'What's Next?' plan to follow up 'No to Failure'. In Southwark there is a commitment to build on the new Lyndhurst Dyslexia Centre with its training facilities, and to have a specialist in every school.

Long term, cost effective, sustainable solutions

In order to have effective inclusion for pupils with dyslexia, the 'No to Failure' Steering Group believes that vital resources of finance, time and effort will best be spent on 'skilling up' professionals in schools so that they can bring their knowledge, skills and experience to successive generations of pupils.

'No to Failure' has communicated and demonstrated the need for all teachers and TAs to have dyslexia/SpLD training so that they can identify and properly support pupils with learning difficulties as early as possible, and deliver quality first teaching in the classroom, and personalised teaching to those who need it. The 'value-added' will be that the same teaching techniques and strategies will benefit all pupils.

Specialists are needed to guide provision for pupils with dyslexia/SpLD, to teach some of those with more severe difficulties, and to support staff on a day-to-day basis to ensure that good practice for pupils with dyslexia/SpLD occurs across the curriculum. Specialists are even more important in secondary school where it is assumed that pupils have established literacy skills sufficient to access the curriculum, and where teachers are not trained, nor expected, to teach those skills.

'No to Failure' believes that the cost effective, sustainable support system for pupils at risk of dyslexia/SpLD demonstrated in the project should now be made available to <u>all</u> schools.

The results and data in the 'No to Failure' final report have been considered by Sir Jim Rose who was asked to undertake a survey of provision for dyslexic pupils.

Reference

Singleton, C. & Wood, R. (2008). No To Failure. In C. Singleton (Ed.) *The Dyslexia Handbook 2008/9*. Bracknell, Berks: British Dyslexia Association (pp. 22-29).

Rosie Wood was SpLD Specialist Advisor to the 'No to Failure' Project. She was formerly Director of the Helen Arkell Dyslexia Centre.

Specialist Dyslexia Teaching

The British Dyslexia Association Quality Mark: towards a dyslexia friendly society

Kate Saunders

Imagine a society where the early identification of dyslexic difficulties was built into the education system as standard. Where children who experienced difficulty with the acquisition of written language skills were identified in Years 1 and 2 at school (from about 5 years of age) and given extra 'booster' group help (e.g. in a ratio of 4:1 pupils to teacher/teaching assistant) for phonics and writing skills, as appropriate to their needs. For some children this would be enough for them to 'catch up'. For others a further, well structured multi-sensory one-to-one written language teaching programme would be necessary.

Imagine that information on dyslexia, and appropriate support, were available for parents in all schools, and that schools were keen to work in positive partnerships with parents to support these pupils.

Imagine that as part of their initial teacher training all classroom teachers acquired a good working knowledge of dyslexia identification, understanding, dyslexia friendly teaching techniques for the classroom, how to make classrooms dyslexia friendly environments, and when to set up additional interventions.

In addition to this, imagine that all schools had at least one teacher on staff who was dyslexia-trained to at least ATS (Approved Teacher Status) level (this is consistent with OCR Level 5). This teacher would assist with identification, support dyslexia friendly classroom practices, carry out one-to-one teaching, set up well structured, multi-sensory teaching programmes and support strategies for teaching assistants, monitor progress, and refine provision accordingly. Clusters of schools would also have access to an AMBDA (Associate Member of the BDA) level dyslexia trained teacher (this is consistent with OCR Level 7). Schools would access the assessment, teaching programme advice and, where necessary, demonstration of one-to-one teaching skills of these AMBDA teachers for those children who are felt to show some severe difficulties. The assessment and advisory skills of educational psychologists would also be available for the more severe cases. Throughout, targets would be set with the aim of enabling individuals to reach their potential, progress would be carefully monitored and programmes adjusted accordingly, in line with the needs of the individual.

The emphasis would be on providing quite intensive help as early as possible to reduce the potential impact of dyslexic difficulties. Intensive one-to-one help would be available for up to one hour daily in schools, where appropriate. In-class teaching assistant support, appropriate to the needs of the individual, would also be available. Where full-time specialist dyslexia provision was considered necessary, education services would enter into this sooner rather than later (ideally in the primary years), in the hope that the improvements made would enable the child to re-enter mainstream education at secondary level. Imagine that the education system ensured that no dyslexic individual left school without functional literacy skills.

Consider if boroughs and children's services were enabled to work in partnership with local and national charities, special educational needs organisations, fundraisers, companies and parents in a positive way. Envisage that funds, training, expertise, resources and personnel from these groups could contribute to supporting pupils with special educational needs in the education system to help meet the real level of need.

Imagine if appropriate access arrangements for examinations and assistive technology was available for all dyslexic individuals (where appropriate), at school, in post 16 years education and in employment. Imagine that all companies and government sponsored organisations adopted a dyslexia friendly approach throughout the organisation. This would be reflected in reasonable adjustments in the work place and lack of discrimination in their selection and promotion practices (in line with the Disability Discrimination Act (DDA) 2005).

Envisage a society where the general understanding of dyslexia would be as a specific learning *difference*, where individuals with dyslexia were respected and acknowledged for their strengths and abilities, and understood and supported for their difficulties. Imagine a society where successful individuals with dyslexia were happy to declare it, providing positive role models for others. Picture a society where saying 'I am dyslexic' was not seen as a negative statement, but rather an expression of difference. Imagine that on hearing this, other people would be interested in the individual's potential strengths, rather than focusing only on potential weaknesses.

The most wonderful thing about this vision of a dyslexia friendly society is that all of it is achievable.

What is required to turn it into reality is vision and commitment from people in all aspects of society who are willing to play an active part in making it happen.

A tremendously exciting aspect of working in this field is the opportunity to meet many such people. People with energy and drive, pushing forward their organisations to bring about positive change for the benefit of dyslexic individuals. These amazing people are in our schools, further/higher education colleges, universities, criminal justice system, companies and government sponsored organisations. Often they have personal experience of dyslexia, either directly themselves, through family members or through working with individuals with dyslexia.

They know what a tremendous difference organisations becoming dyslexia friendly can make for individuals with dyslexia. They are changing society from within, and changing it for the better.

The BDA would like to thank and celebrate these people and organisations for the work they do, and encourage others to follow their lead.

The British Dyslexia Association Quality Mark

The BDA Quality Mark provides an excellent mechanism for bringing about effective change in all areas of society. The Quality Mark requires the whole organisation to become dyslexia friendly in policies and practices. It is recognised as the bench mark standard in the UK. Organisations that achieve the BDA Quality Mark can use the BDA Quality Mark logo on their stationery and marketing material.

Dyslexia friendly education

The BDA Quality Mark is a whole school approach. The BDA recognises that the majority of dyslexics will spend most of their time in school in mainstream classrooms, being taught by non-specialist tutors. Therefore it is important that general classroom environments are dyslexia friendly and employ appropriate teaching methods, in addition to schools providing specialist teaching programmes for one-to-one and small group intervention work.

Sixteen Local Education Authorities (LEAs)/children's services, six colleges of further education and seven schools in the UK have already achieved the BDA Quality Mark award. Where LEAs/children's services have achieved the award, many of these have initiated programmes for schools in their area whereby the schools have gone through a local LEA/children's service Quality Mark process, based around and adapted from the BDA standards and criteria. The influence of the Quality Mark has, therefore, been widespread and it has been a force for good in many schools and for very many dyslexic pupils.

An additional 10 schools, 19 LEAs/children's services and 14 further education colleges are currently working towards the BDA Quality Mark. The BDA would like to encourage other educational establishments to register for the award, including post- 16 years training establishments and universities. The specific standards for each sector of education are different, as appropriate to the setting. However, the basic structure of the process is the same.

Schools registering for the BDA Quality Mark carry out a self-audit against a set of standards provided by the BDA. These standards cover all areas of school life including:

1. Leadership and management
2. Quality of teaching and learning

3. Creating a climate for learning
4. Partnership and liaison with parents, carers, governors and other concerned parties

From the audit the school identifies those areas which they need to develop further, and draws up an action plan of how to do this. This will commonly include some additional training of staff in quality first dyslexia friendly teaching and support (for teachers and teaching assistants). Schools should have systems for early identification of possible dyslexic difficulties and deliver effective intervention programs as early as possible. They should also work to build the self-esteem of dyslexic individuals.

Having implemented the action plan, schools prepare a "Record of Evidence" to show that they are now meeting each of the BDA Quality Mark criteria, and submit this to the BDA. The BDA will ask to see some of this evidence in advance of a verification visit. At the verification visit the BDA will carry out observations and interviews with a range of school personnel, pupils, governors and parents. They also ask to see any further evidence that they might require to show that the school is meeting the BDA Quality Mark criteria.

If the criteria are met, the BDA Dyslexia Friendly Quality Mark is awarded. If the school has further work to do to meet the standards, the verification report will outline what is required, then the school can re-apply for verification when they feel they have met all the standards. Schools generally have two years to complete this process, and once awarded they are re-verified every three years to continue to embed good practice.

Teachers report that going through the BDA Quality Mark process helps not only the dyslexic pupils, but pupils with other special needs as well. There is evidence that awarded primary schools show decreasing numbers of children failing in reading at the end of primary school. Pupils report that they feel people understand their dyslexia more, staff and pupils help them more, they feel able to ask for help, and their reading and writing skills have improved. The pupils know that they are not on their own in having dyslexic difficulties and they are helped to understand their potential strengths. Schools work to build the self-esteem of dyslexic pupils (eg. through assemblies showing positive role-models who are dyslexic). One primary school boy, when asked what difference the school becoming dyslexia friendly had made to him, said, "I can smile now". That's a difference worth making.

Companies/Government sponsored organisations

A very exciting recent development has been the launch of the BDA Quality Mark for organisations. This has been enthusiastically received. Employers are keen to have a mechanism that has regard to ensuring that they fulfil their legal requirements under the DDA (2005) to make reasonable adjustments for disabled employees, and most dyslexic individuals fall into this category.

Companies registering for the BDA Quality Mark review their policies and practices internally against a written BDA set of dyslexia friendly standards. They then draw up an action plan, with a lead person within the organisation ensuring that the action points are addressed across the company. The BDA Quality Mark support staff are available to offer advice and direction at all stages.

Northease Manor School

Changing lives, building confidence, creating independent citizens

A small Independent School for pupils aged 10 to 17 with Specific Learning Difficulties including Dyslexia and Dyspraxia

"Northease Manor is an excellent school"

"Outstanding value for money"
"Curriculum is outstanding"

"Progress that pupils made is outstanding"
Source: Ofsted - July 2007

"Boarding and Care are outstanding"
Source: Ofsted - November 2007

- ✓ For Girls and Boys aged 10 to 17

- ✓ Weekly Boarding or Day placements

- ✓ On-site Speech and Language Therapy and Occupational Therapy

- ✓ Individual learning programmes in small classes where everyone is valued

- ✓ Access for all to GCSE examinations with highly successful results record

To find out more, or to arrange an appointment to visit us, please contact the Secretary:
Northease Manor School, Rodmell, Lewes, East Sussex, BN7 3EY
Tel: 01273 472915 Fax: 01273 472202 E-mail: office@northease.co.uk
Or visit our website: www.northease.co.uk
Registered Charity no. 307005

Once the company feels they are meeting the standards, they complete a record stating what evidence they have for each item and where it is located. A BDA verifier carries out a verification visit reviewing a sample of evidence, conducting interviews and requesting further evidence where appropriate. If successful, the organisation is awarded the BDA Quality Mark by means of a certificate and they can then use the BDA Quality Mark logo on company material.

The first companies to register for the BDA Quality Mark are from the construction and training sectors. There is also interest in the Quality Mark from a number of other sectors, including technology, industry, health, police and service-based organisations.

Often within these organisations there are inspirational individuals who are willing to drive this initiative for the benefit of dyslexic employees and customers. It is important for businesses and service industries to realise that 10% of the population is dyslexic to some extent, and this may include 10% of the employees of the organisation as well as 10% of the customers. Becoming dyslexia friendly is likely to increase the effectiveness of those employees and the appeal of products or services to those customers. In these competitive times, this could help to give a company an important edge. Organisations can also benefit from releasing the creative ability and potential of their dyslexic employees for the benefit of the company.

The vision of a dyslexia friendly society is an achievable one. All it needs is for people to take action.

For further information on the BDA Quality Mark and related INSET/ training, please contact:

Joanne Gregory
Quality Mark Development Manager
01656 724 585
07786 071020
e-mail: qualitymark@bdadyslexia.org.uk
Quality Mark details: www.bdadyslexia.org.uk

Dr Kate Saunders is Education and Policy Director at the BDA

If you are arrested remember that dyslexia & stress can mean you present poorly!

Are you dyslexic / disabled?

If the Police want to interview you,
ask for help <u>before</u> the interview starts.

It may be too late if you tell someone later!

Tell the Custody Sergeant and your Solicitor.

Show them this card to help explain.

Call 077 9988 7984 any time

(We will switch to a landline as soon as we can!)

Need more A-cards? www.psychologist.co.uk/a-card   PTO

Cut out this card, carry it with you.

We can give Police & Solicitors advice BEFORE interview.

We can produce reports about you for use in Court.

Need information or more A-cards?
0844 357 8307

North Ayrshire's developing approach to identifying and meeting the needs of learners with dyslexia

Allan Cowieson

Defining the problem in North Ayrshire

What concerned parents? Lack of good, sustained progress in developing literacy skills in their children, and children who were becoming increasingly unhappy in school. Historically, most parents who contacted North Ayrshire schools with concerns that their child might have dyslexia were unhappy with the response they received. Schools' responses were frequently interpreted as off-hand, poorly informed, hesitant and, in the worst cases, evasive.

What concerned teachers? The feeling that while they were identifying children with severe literacy difficulties, they had no framework within which to identify these difficulties as dyslexia. Teachers were also concerned because they did not know whether they were allowed to use the term 'dyslexia' in discussions with learners and their parents/carers.

Planning the response

In 2004, the education authority felt that it had to intervene to address these concerns and to ensure that all of its schools were well informed, well trained and well resourced to meet the needs of learners with dyslexia.

The first stage of our intervention involved determining whether the British Psychological Society's definition of dyslexia could be used in schools to identify learners who would require additional and alternative types of support to master literacy skills. The BPS definition states that:

"Dyslexia is evident when accurate and fluent word reading and/or spelling develops very incompletely or with great difficulty. This focuses on literacy learning at the 'word level' and implies that the problem is severe and persistent despite appropriate learning opportunities. It provides the basis for a staged process of assessment through teaching" (The British Psychological Society, 1999).

The authority elected to use this definition as it had been developed by that body governing the professional practice of all chartered psychologists working in the UK.

Over an 18 month period, 22 Support for Learning teachers worked with the North Ayrshire Quality Improvement Officer (QIO) to develop: (1) the use of the definition in their work with teachers; and (2) the use of the Cognitive Profiling System (CoPS) and LUCID Assessment System for Schools (LASS Junior – see www.lucid-research.com/index.htm) to take a closer look at specific areas of processing difficulty. CoPS and LASS Junior are diagnostic packages that provide a profile of performance across areas such as short-term visual and auditory memory, the ability to break words down into syllables, phonological sensitivity, spelling, and reading.

Thirty primary schools were involved in this study which was evaluated by parents, children and teachers. Evaluation was conducted through a series of meetings to discuss curricular assessments alongside software profiles. The results were positive, confirming a strong match between pupils already identified as having curriculum-based literacy difficulties and those who achieved a significant dyslexia profile on the software assessments[1]. This assured us that the BPS definition could be used to identify dyslexia through normal classroom-based assessment, and a decision was made to involve all of the authority's 62 mainstream schools.

The QIO and the authority's Principal Psychologist worked together on an information booklet for parents and professionals (see link at the end of the chapter), and on a development strategy for all schools in relation to dyslexia; this involved informing, training and resourcing.

During 2005-6, Dr Chris Singleton (Lucid Research/University of Hull) was a regular visitor to the authority to work with school staff, educational psychologists, and parents. During these visits, a great deal of effort went into unpacking the BPS's definition of dyslexia. Basically, the definition was interpreted as:

> *"Where a child/young person and the teacher both have to work much harder than most of the children in a class, and where literacy skills are still incomplete and poorly retained, then the child is registered as being dyslexic. Schools will inform children/young people and their parents/carers of their earliest concerns and will use the term dyslexia in their discussions."*

Further work went into understanding how this definition could be used to empower teachers to identify, at the earliest opportunity, where children were failing to master sound

1 The software programmes have been tested extensively to determine how well children generally perform on the individual measures. The result of this testing provides 'normative data' for each measure. Following each assessment, the software then creates a grid to show how well the child being assessed performs in relation to these normative data.

literacy skills. This involved matching what is described in the definition with real-life examples that would be readily understood by teachers drawing on their own experiences. In Scotland, many teachers started work in an educational climate where they were discouraged from using the term 'dyslexia'. One of the hardest aspects of implementing the strategy has been to persuade them to use the term readily, openly, and in a well-informed way.

How did we do it?

Development work was undertaken with staff in individual schools. This involved whole-school consultation, and running whole-day and twilight dyslexia training courses through the authority's staff development catalogue. These courses were (and continue to be) delivered by the QIO and by educational psychologists with an emphasis on the early and confident identification of dyslexia.

Additional support for learning

The Additional Support for Learning Act (2004) places a statutory duty on local authorities in Scotland to ensure that children who need additional educational support have their needs identified and met as early as possible. To meet the demands of this Act we implemented the following staged intervention:

Stage 1
Children who need only a little help receive this in-class from teachers and classroom assistants. There is an emphasis on matching teaching and learning strategies to the individual needs and strengths of learners (i.e. differentiating the curriculum) to prevent dyslexic learners from becoming

discouraged and overwhelmed. So, for example, peer support, paired reading and structured group work have been developed.

A range of resources has been purchased to target specific areas of processing weakness; these include software packages to address short-term memory and auditory difficulties (e.g. *Memory Booster* and *Earobics*), and phonological difficulties (e.g. *Lexia 5* and *WordShark*)[2]. For some primary schools where there were high levels of dyslexia referrals, whole-class sets of *Reading Rods* were distributed.

Teachers maintain an assessment and monitoring sheet to track progress, and even from this stage, teachers discuss their concerns with the children and their parents.

Stage 2
This is a higher level of direct support provided by the teacher and Support for Learning staff. Teachers are encouraged to take a closer look at the specific areas of processing difficulty faced by individual children. To this end, all primary schools are now equipped with CoPS and LASS Junior, secondary schools with LASS Secondary. These software programmes are not used to diagnose dyslexia – identification will already have taken place at an earlier stage through careful assessment around the BPS definition – but to identify which areas need to be addressed so that programmes of work can be tailored to individual needs.

Learners then have access to resources that target their specific difficulties, e.g. *Phonix* and *Sentifix* offer tactile, multi-coloured approaches to word and sentence building; *Phonological Awareness Training* and games such as *What's GNU?* are

2 Links to suppliers of all the curriculum materials and packages mentioned here and later is given at the end of this chapter.

used to develop phonological skills; the *Where's Wally?* books promote skills in organised searching for picture-based information.

Stage 3
This stage requires input from two or more agencies working together to meet a child's/young person's needs. Around dyslexia, this joint support might involve a Speech and Language Therapist, a qualified support teacher and the class teacher.

Stage 4
Provision at stage 4 is likely to be long-term and to involve specialist educational placements. Only children and young people with very complex needs are deemed to require such placements.

For learners identified as having severe, long-term literacy difficulties, laptop computers may be issued with tailored software packages to offer long-term support. Assessment is undertaken to establish what types of software might be best suited to each individual.

North Ayrshire currently has more than 1,800 dyslexic children who are registered at different stages on the intervention framework (Stages 1 – 3).

What has changed over the past three years?

The local authority supports a centralised approach to listening to parents'/carers' concerns. Since the dyslexia approaches have become embedded in what schools do, there has been a significant drop in the number of parents who contact the authority about their concerns. From a high before implementing the project of between 20 – 30 referrals to the authority per year, present rates have levelled out at around three – four per year. Schools are now <u>almost always</u> the initiating point of referral, teachers have become much more comfortable with the use of the term dyslexia and with staged intervention, and the majority of pupils have their needs identified early.

Where are we now?

Much of the strategy has been implemented over the past three years during which the authority has continued to focus on certain priorities:

- to increase teacher sensitivity to the reading, writing and spelling difficulties faced by some pupils
- to speed up the process of dyslexia identification and assessment by nursery staff and classroom teachers
- to involve children and their parents/carers at the earliest stage of concern over literacy development
- to establish careful and clear processes for monitoring progress, and for evaluating the adequacy of the support packages being implemented

Where do we want to go next?

Our first priority is to build on the many examples of good practice that have developed in schools over the past three years. This will involve making high-quality provision across all schools in the authority. We do still have occasional requests from parents, and when it does happen the QIO with responsibility for Additional Support for Learning, or the school's educational psychologist will work with both parents and the school to ensure that a child's needs are identified and met. Where it is necessary to do so, the local authority will provide additional resources to the school to help address the child's difficulties.

Identification of difficulties in the nursery

In early-years education, the first step is to work with local Speech and Language Therapy services to establish a framework for identifying children in the nursery who may be at risk for dyslexia. Following development of the assessment framework, extensive training will be offered to staff in all early years centres.

Improving communication and the involvement of parents/carers

Children in Scotland, a charity supported by the Scottish Government, was commissioned to survey levels of pupil and parent/carer satisfaction with arrangements for identifying and addressing additional support needs. On the whole, children and parents/carers felt that adequate support was in place, and that school staff were very helpful; this was reflected in the high levels of expressed satisfaction (80%). However, there were still areas of concern, such as the need to improve the quality of information provided to parents/carers, to begin the process of communication much earlier, and to increase parents'/carers' participation in educational planning. These concerns have been used to develop an action plan to improve services further through additional guidance and training.

New initiatives at secondary school stage

Changes in examination procedures from the Scottish Qualifications Authority mean that young people sitting national examinations can now do so on-line. The availability of digital exam papers means that text can be read aloud (via text-to-speech software) and answers can be typed or dictated on to computer.

For all the authority's secondary schools, site licences for *Read and Write Gold* have been purchased to stimulate the development of support materials and strategies across the curriculum. The software will enable, for example, whole texts and workbooks to be downloaded on to MP3/4 players for use at home and in class.

Changes in the copyright legislation in Scotland (which previously only covered people with sensory or physical disabilities) now mean that the needs of children and young people with dyslexia are also being met. To this end, any child who has a difficulty accessing text can now have full texts provided in ways that are accessible for them. A national "Books for All" electronic warehouse of texts that have been altered into Braille, large print and PDF format (for use with software that can read the text to the child) is being developed.

Training for secondary school staff is being provided by *Communication, Access, Literacy and Learning (CALL) Scotland*, an educational unit funded by the Scottish Government to develop the use of technology in educational settings to address the needs of all learners requiring additional support. An ICT specialist from *CALL Scotland* is working in secondary schools to help teachers to develop accessible curriculum materials that ensure that dyslexic learners can access and produce text. So far, four days have been spent with staff from each school.

It is hoped that initiatives like this will increase not only the support available to children and young people but also their experience of independence in learning.

The journey is not yet over. North Ayrshire is committed to continuous improvement of all its services, and we look forward to the next stage of developing support for learners with dyslexia.

Reference

Dyslexia, Literacy and Psychological Assessment: Report by a working party of the Division of Educational and Child Psychologists (1999). The British Psychological Society, Leicester

Links to additional resources

To access North Ayrshire's Dyslexia booklet: (1) Google 'North Ayrshire Council' (2) Click 'Education and Learning' (3) Type 'dyslexia' into the search box (4) Click 'Go'

The following resources are given as examples of the type and range available in all North Ayrshire schools:

Memory Booster by Lucid
    www.memorybooster.com
Earobics by Houghton Mifflin Harcourt Learning Technology
    www.earobics.com
Lexia5 by Lexia Learning Systems
    www.donjohnston.co.uk
WordShark by White Space Ltd.
    www.wordshark.co.uk
Reading Rods by Learning Resources

www.learningresources.co.uk
Phonix by Sue Palmer
www.suepalmer.co.uk
Sentifix by Sue Palmer
www.suepalmer.co.uk
Phonological Awareness Training (PAT) by University
College London
www.ucl.ac.uk/educational-psychology/cpd/pat.htm
What's GNU? by The Happy Puzzle Company
www.happypuzzle.co.uk
Where's Wally? by The Happy Puzzle Company
www.happypuzzle.co.uk

Allan Cowieson is Quality Improvement Officer for North
Ayrshire Council

Stupid? Lazy? Dyslexic? Student teachers' attitudes about dyslexia

Ruth Gwernan-Jones and Robert Burden

Why do teachers teach the way they do?

Icek Ajzen, in his *Theory of Planned Behaviour* (TPB; 1991) proposed that people act according to their personal beliefs, the beliefs of those around them, and the perceptions of how much control or power they have in a particular situation. Therefore, the personal attitudes toward dyslexia of teachers, the attitudes toward dyslexia in local school cultures and our wider culture, and teachers' perceived levels of competence are important aspects of how dyslexic pupils are supported in schools. Because little research has looked at newly qualified teachers' attitudes toward dyslexia, as well as their perceptions of their own competence in teaching dyslexic pupils, we decided to survey student teachers and focus on these particular facets of why future teachers are likely to teach the way they do.

Attitudes about dyslexia in local school cultures and our wider culture

The conclusion by many academics that dyslexia is an umbrella term for a number of different phenomena, on varying continuums of severity (see Figure 1), makes sense of some of the confusion and contradiction that has shadowed dyslexia during its relatively brief, 100 year career. Dyslexia is sometimes described with the Indian story of five blind men and an elephant, where each man touches a different part of the elephant, describes it, then argues with the other four men about whose description is correct. The case of dyslexia is

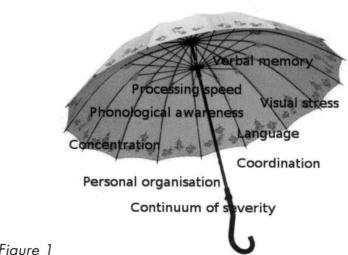

Figure 1

even more complex because the shape of the 'elephant' is a little different for every dyslexic person.

This lack of agreement amongst experts in the field about what exactly dyslexia is, has contributed to an initial reluctance within our educational system to take on board information about it. In addition, much research on the stigma and negative effects of labelling within education has led to a reluctance by teachers to 'label' children for fear of harming them.

At the same time, the profound impact that failing at school can have on the individual, and the links such experiences have with identity, means that for dyslexic people (and those who care about them) dyslexia is a highly emotive topic. Impersonal negative attitudes about dyslexia can have a personally negative impact on a dyslexic person.

Therefore, there is a potent mixture of perspectives in our culture from which to draw when attempting to understand dyslexia. For this reason, the attitudes that teachers entering the profession hold about dyslexia is particularly uncertain, but relevant for the reasons explained above.

The survey

We developed a survey composed of statements partly based on the principles of TPB, as well as attitudes we had heard expressed by teachers, parents and dyslexic pupils, views expressed in the media, and current research literature about dyslexia. Because of limitations of length, we will only be reporting some of the results from this survey here. Further details can be found in Gwernan-Jones & Burden (in press).

In total, 404 primary and secondary students on a Post Graduate Certificate in Education (PGCE) course responded to the survey. Their mean age was 26, with a range from 20 to 55 years. We do not claim the respondents are representative of all UK student teachers; however, the students at this particular university come from all parts of the UK, and therefore can be seen to be reasonably indicative of attitudes of teachers currently entering the profession.

Student teachers' beliefs about the existence of dyslexia

Statement 1 was included to gauge the influence of a Channel 4 television programme *The Dyslexia Myth* (2005) on student teachers' attitudes. The responses to Statement 1 show that over 90% of respondents strongly disagreed (69%) or disagreed (24%) with the statement 'I think dyslexia is a myth'.

Statement 2 was based on overheard remarks by practising teachers, as well as comments by dyslexic adults of things that adults had said to them during their childhoods. The student

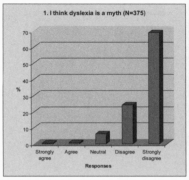 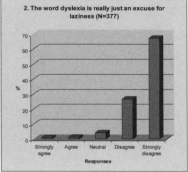

Figure 2

teachers responded similarly in statement 2 to their response in statement 1; over 90% of student teacher respondents strongly disagreed (67.4%) or disagreed (26.5%) with 'The word dyslexia is really just an excuse for laziness'.

The response by the student teachers to both these statements demonstrates that the vast majority believe there is a condition, dyslexia, which is not to be dismissed. In TPB terms, the negative perceptions of dyslexia represented by these two statements have not strongly influenced the student teachers' beliefs.

Student teachers' beliefs about the potential of dyslexic pupils

Statement 3 was chosen to gauge the belief of student teachers about dyslexic pupils' prospects for success. Their responses show that a large majority (86%) strongly disagreed (58%) or disagreed (28%) that 'Dyslexic children often do not succeed as adults'.

Statement 4 was chosen to see whether or not student teachers linked difficulties with reading and writing to low intelligence.

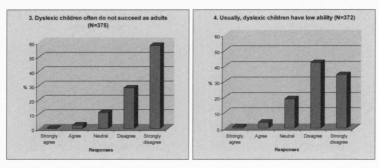

Figure 3

Again, a large majority (76%) strongly disagreed (34%) or disagreed (42%) that 'Usually, dyslexic children have low ability'.

Both responses demonstrate that most of these student teachers believed in the potential of dyslexic pupils. In TPB terms, this would suggest that these teachers will believe their dyslexic students are intelligent and have the ability to succeed in their future lives and careers.

Student teachers' perceptions of their own competence

Statement 5 was included to gauge student teachers' perceptions of their own competence. The majority (58%) agreed (49%) or strongly agreed (9%) that 'I feel confident that I could support a dyslexic child's learning'. This response is not so univocal as responses to the first four statements; almost a quarter of respondents were unsure (24%) and a smaller number disagreed (18%). However, this suggests that many student teachers had a strong sense of competence in their ability to support dyslexic pupils.

Statement 6 was included to discover whether the student

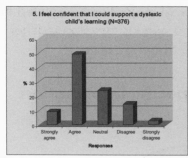 

Figure 4

teachers desired more training about dyslexia. The responses to this statement were once again univocal, with the vast majority (91%) agreeing (56%) or strongly agreeing (35%) that 'I feel more training should be given to teachers about dyslexia'.

One might view responses to statements 5 and 6 as somewhat contradictory, since the majority feel confident they could support dyslexic children, while the vast majority feel the need for more training about dyslexia. It may be that their teacher education programme developed the student teachers' general sense of confidence to the degree that although they had not received very much specific information about dyslexia, most felt they could adapt and differentiate to support a range of children inclusively. In this case, they could still respond with agreement to statement 6 without contradiction.

In TPB terms, the sense of competence many student teachers express suggests they have a strong sense of behavioural control; this means they are likely to act upon the positive beliefs about dyslexia they expressed in statements 1-4. However, this final aspect of TPB, a sense of competence, is one that could be developed more to prepare teachers to respond to dyslexic pupils in positive ways. Both the minority of student teachers who did not feel confident about their ability to support dyslexic pupils, and the vast majority who wanted more training about dyslexia, indicate a need to develop teacher education to be more informative about dyslexia.

Teaching practice and specific information about dyslexia

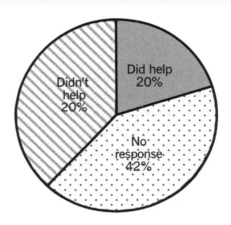

The chart above details responses to the open-ended question, 'Please describe how your experiences during teaching practice have developed your understanding of dyslexia'. Only 1 in 5 student teachers responded by describing ways in which teaching practice supported their understanding of dyslexia. Of these, few made explicit reference to helpful skills or strategies. This supports the discussion of Statements 5 and 6 above, that although teacher training developed student teachers' confidence in supporting pupils generally, they were given little information about supporting dyslexic pupils specifically.

Conclusion

Coming back to *The Theory of Planned Behaviour*, this study has shown that the student teachers surveyed hold positive attitudes about the existence of dyslexia and the potential of dyslexic pupils to succeed. This may indicate the wane of dismissive attitudes about dyslexia such that it is a 'middle-class name for stupid' and 'just laziness', and instead signal that a new breed of freshly qualified teachers is entering the teaching profession with reformulated, positive attitudes about dyslexia. That many student teachers felt a high sense of competence makes it likely that their intention to act positively towards dyslexic pupils will be carried through.

However, a minority of student teachers felt ambiguous or lacked confidence in their ability to support dyslexic pupils' learning, and the vast majority desired additional training about dyslexia. Both signal the need to develop teacher training to provide additional information about support for dyslexic pupils.

References

Dispatches: The Dyslexia Myth (2005). *Tonight with Trevor MacDonald,* Channel 4 television.

Ajzen, I. (1991). The Theory of Planned Behaviour. *Organisational Behaviour and Human Decision Process, 50,* 179-211.

Gwernan-Jones, R. & Burden, R. L. (in press). *Are they just lazy?* Student teachers' attitudes about dyslexia. *Dyslexia.*

Ruth Gwernan-Jones is a PhD student at the School of Education, University of Exeter, working on a thesis about the experience of being dyslexic. Her PhD supervisor is **Robert Burden**, who is Emeritus Professor of Applied Educational Psychology at Exeter. Both are BDA trustees.

Postgraduate specialist training for teachers of SpLD – impact and e-learning

Anne Sheddick

Specialist postgraduate teacher training by e-learning

Dyslexia Action has developed an acclaimed innovative e-learning course for teachers across primary, secondary, further, higher and other education settings to train specialist dyslexia teachers to postgraduate (PG) level. The course can be accessed from any computer worldwide and students can study the course from wherever they live and work. At the start of the course students attend an intensive residential induction course and the remainder of their studies take place online. Practical teaching and assessment work and assignments link directly to their current employment or voluntary work.

The current educational landscape and Dyslexia Action's work

This is an especially interesting time to be considering what it means to be a specialist teacher in the field of dyslexia and SpLD, and the training that is required to become such a specialist. It is also a time when the requirement to understand how to meet the needs of dyslexic learners has been given a welcome boost as all teachers are required to undertake continuing professional development (CPD).

It is clear that the ground is shifting for the teaching profession in some fundamental ways. A key change is that there is now a clear expectation that:

- teachers will continue with professional training throughout their professional lives
- meeting the needs of pupils with SEN is a fundamental part of training
- qualifications for 'specialist teachers' will be at master's level

The Teaching Development Agency's (TDA) recent launch of Professional Standards for teachers defines pathways for career progression, while performance review processes provide a framework for specialist career progression. CPD and PG level courses are integral to this process.

The Inclusion Development Programme (IDP), launched by the Department of Children, Schools and Families, is a CPD programme which all teachers and learning assistants in English schools are expected to engage with during the current and forthcoming academic year. For the dyslexia strand, the aim is to ensure that everyone understands, and is working towards, meeting the needs of dyslexic learners in the classroom. Dyslexia Action were the main authors of the IDP Dyslexia strand of the programme and are now offering a national programme of CPD to support schools with the associated training.

Dyslexia Action is also working with over 50 schools to deliver a project called 'Partnership for Literacy'. This involves specialist teachers working alongside teachers and learning assistants for a specified period in their schools whilst the teachers and learning assistants develop and deliver teaching programmes for learners falling behind with literacy who may also be dyslexic. Evaluation of this programme by the University of Durham has shown that it has had a very positive impact on the learners and the professional development of the teachers.

Master's level training

Currently the TDA supports the professional postgraduate training at master's level through the Postgraduate Professional Development (PPD) Programme. This supports universities to work in partnership with local authorities, the voluntary sector, and other relevant organisations to deliver specialist postgraduate training for teachers.

Dyslexia Action offers a postgraduate certificate and diploma validated by the University of York as part of this programme. Over the last two years Dyslexia Action has developed a blended e-learning model for delivery of these courses. About 180 teachers are registered on the postgraduate courses at any one time. This makes this the largest course offering education and training for practical specialist teaching and assessment linked to the necessary theoretical understanding and reflective enquiry required for master's level study.

Why blended e-learning?

There are several key reasons for offering a blended e-learning model.

1. The first is that it is essential to offer flexible options so that career teachers can manage advanced CPD around busy professional lives and family commitments. Teachers studying on the course come from around the country and indeed the world (we have had students from 18 countries studying with us on the programme over the last two years), and are working in many settings both full- and part-time, in

primary, secondary, early years, prisons and offender institutions, colleges and universities.

2. The second is that e-learning offers the opportunity to build sustainable communities of learning and practice amongst aspiring teachers in this field. These individuals all work and share professional experiences together in the course of becoming specialist teachers.

3. E-learning is delivered via a web-based learning environment called Moodle. This means not only that an extensive range of course materials is available online but that the learning is enhanced by tutors and students working together on an ongoing basis, discussing ideas together. Topics for study each week are accompanied by various learning tasks, and tutors and students discuss each other's ideas and contributions so that ideas are shared and developed throughout the course – students and tutors learn from each other.

Course structure and induction school

Early on in the course students are required to attend an intensive four day residential induction school. During the induction, intensive work is done so that students are introduced to the teaching programme that they will use to develop the structured multi-sensory techniques they need to work with during their teaching practice. They are also introduced to the assessment materials so they know how the tests they will use work, and can practise and become confident in using them.

During the induction school students get to know one another and their tutors so that thereafter they can continue to study online throughout the course. They are a member of a small tutor group of up to six students with their personal tutor, and also of the larger class that is their cohort of up to 60, working with up to 15 specialist education and psychology tutors. Particular modules involve discussions and activities conducted by specialist tutors and psychologists online.

This structure ensures that all students are supported by tutors and their peers on an ongoing basis 24/7. Working on the e-learning Dyslexia Action course is completely different from some distance learning courses because there is always someone available online to answer a question, offer support, comment on ideas and extend the learning.

Practical teaching and assessment work are also reviewed and discussed online. Students upload lesson plans, evaluations and teaching materials onto the Moodle, and receive feedback on a weekly basis on their lesson plans, materials and lesson evaluations from their tutors. The same process is undertaken with assessments. Students send their tutors videos of teaching and assessments for comment and review. Finally, the teaching programme and assessments are compiled together in teaching diary and case study assignments for course assessments.

More theoretical elements of the course are taught through delivery of online lectures, interactive PowerPoint presentations and group tasks. These are linked to relevant readings and current research. There is an emphasis on reflection, critical analysis, engagement with current new ideas and research in the field, and enquiry, as would be expected of a master's level course. The online discussions associated with these modules always link back to the practical teaching and assessment requirements of dyslexic learners so students develop an evidence-based approach to their professional work.

Impact of continuing professional development

The TDA has defined 'good CPD' as professional learning which has an impact at three levels:

- the individual teacher
- the learner
- the professional institution/ environment

The Dyslexia Action PG course is designed to meet these criteria and to require students to evaluate and record the impact of the course and its activities at these three levels. Each student records their development throughout the course in their own personal blog space on the Moodle. They can choose to share part or all of this with peers and tutors as they wish. They are required to review their progress and conduct an impact analysis as part of their final assignment for the course.

It is truly inspiring for students and tutors alike to review the impact of the training of specialist teachers at this point. It is clear that the PG course we offer has immense impact on developing the confidence and skills of individual teachers who study and complete the course successfully.

Most diploma graduates gain promotion and move into roles where they have the opportunity to act as change agents in their environment, training other teachers and learning assistants, improving the policy and practice in their schools and colleges. There is no doubt at all that the effort required to complete this demanding course repays students handsomely in professional and personal development.

Community of practice for specialist teachers

The ambitious aim of the Dyslexia Action e-learning course team was not just that we would teach a course that produced world class specialist teachers, but also that we would create an enduring community of professional specialist teachers who would continue to work together and develop beyond the life of the course.

We know we have achieved the former aim because of the endorsements of our students, the external examiner and the University of York. We know we have achieved the latter aim because our past graduates have asked us to continue to provide them with Moodle so they can continue to work, share and learn together online.

The future

The master's in Teaching and Learning currently under development is planned to enable all teachers to gain a master's level qualification by 2017. This qualification is expected to have SpLD specialist options in the third stage.

The Rose Review on the teaching of learners with SpLD also points to the importance of training for teachers and teaching assistants who help dyslexic learners, and the development of training at PG level for SENCOs and specialist teachers.

We look forward to supporting the growth of the community of specialist teachers in the UK and beyond through postgraduate education and e-learning for the benefit of dyslexic learners worldwide through our current course and new initiatives in CPD for teachers and other practitioners in the field of dyslexia.

Anne Sheddick is Head of Training at Dyslexia Action

Dyslexia and the American public school system

Nick Hakiel

This morning my wife, a reading specialist who works with children with dyslexia in private practice, received the phone call which many an educational therapist or parent of a child with dyslexia will be able to relate to. A parent seeking help for a child diagnosed with dyslexia. Like many parents she had initially turned to her public school system only to be told that dyslexia doesn't exist.

In this chapter I intend to review the attitudes of American public schools to students with dyslexia. For the main part, it is not a story which will bring comfort to families whose children have dyslexia. We will review the typical responses by the public education system and the intent of federal legislation to ensure that children with dyslexia receive services in the public school system, and review how that legislative intent has been frustrated. We also map out the strategy most likely to succeed in providing appropriate services to students with dyslexia.

In the United States the history of the relationship between public education and students with dyslexia is long. At the same time that America was moving towards a new model for the education of students with disabilities (the late 1960s), there was a growing debate about dyslexia.

In 1974, landmark legislation was passed by the US Congress in the form of the Individual with Disabilities Education Act (IDEA). In this legislation dyslexia was recognized as a condition that might contribute to a specific learning disability, but it did not recognize dyslexia as a category of disability. This has remained true in subsequent reauthorizations of that legislation.

Not just semantics

This is not just a matter of semantics. It is generally reported by researchers of dyslexia that about 80% of students recognized as having a learning disability have a reading disability, and of those students with a reading disability about 80% are dyslexic, so most students with learning disabilities are in fact, dyslexic.

However, public schools are required to address not a condition of dyslexia, but a reading disability. The dyslexic brain is a brain that processes information differently to the non-dyslexic brain, and this has pervasive and global implications for the educational environment.

Furthermore, most students with dyslexia do not have a reading disability of sufficient severity to qualify for special education. They are therefore often left with no accommodations or supports, and they move through school never realising their academic potential, but not failing enough to trigger additional services.

The big gap

In the US reading instruction is delivered almost universally through one of three models:

- Whole Language – a complex educational philosophy that was dominant through the eighties and nineties; in reading instruction it emphasised literature based learning with a

meaning-based sight word approach
- Direct Instruction of Phonics – this approaches reading instruction by teaching the component phoneme-grapheme associations and building up to word decoding
- Balanced Literacy – an integrative approach which claims to take the best elements of both whole language and phonics

Since the National Reading Panel Report of 2000, Direct Instruction of Phonics has become more common, especially in remedial programs such as Title 1 programs (a massive, federally-funded nationwide academic support program), and of course it has a long history in special education.

Absent from this list is multi-sensory instruction. For nearly 100 years, from the pioneering work of Orton and Gillingham, it has been well-established that the most effective instruction for dyslexic children is multi-sensory. Multi-sensory instruction models are used in the United States, but not to an extent to impact the majority of schools, and there is huge variation state by state.

The models with the highest name recognition are:

- The Slingerland Multisensory Approach – a classroom adaptation of the Orton-Gillingham Approach. Originally created for preventive instruction, it is used today both as a preventive and remedial approach
- The Lindamood Phonemic Sequencing (LiPS) Program - individuals become aware of the mouth actions which produce speech sounds. This awareness becomes the means of verifying sounds within words and enables individuals to become self-correcting in reading, spelling and speech
- The Wilson Reading System – a 12-Step remedial reading

and writing program for individuals with a language-based learning disability. This is based on Orton-Gillingham philosophy and principles and current phonological coding research

There are 50 states that comprise the United States of America, and control of education is at the discretion of each individual state. On average 50% of a state's budget is spent on education, and that is supplemented by a significant share of local property taxes (in my county, 50% of my property taxes are for public schools). Unfortunately, 50 states mean 50 different approaches to the management of dyslexia, or lack thereof.

In 1985 Texas was the first state to pass legislation to provide for the identification and support of students with dyslexia. It remains an outstanding model which is as rigorous as special education law, but the dyslexia program is intentionally completely distinct from the special education process. Any parent or teacher can request a free dyslexia assessment for students in Kindergarten through 2nd Grade (5 to 8 years) who are struggling in reading, writing or spelling. If a student is recognised as having dyslexia, then they receive extensive programming from a dyslexia specialist via a "research based best practices" program designed for children with dyslexia.

That at least is the intent of the system. Far beyond the scope of this chapter is the problem of American public education as a failed bureaucracy. Even where a state has legislated and funded a specific program, it will face the same limitations as all programs in public schools. For years it has been recognised that changes in the school system will not occur unless there is almost total commitment from all members of the educational community to engage in the process of change. Just like every other initiative seeking to improve the quality of

Mark College

is a specialist residential secondary school
for students aged 10 to 19 years with Dyslexia

Mark College has an
international reputation
for its educational work
with dyslexic students.
Its goal is straightforward,
to provide a top class
education for all students.

To help achieve this goal, it has superb facilities and staff whose
skills and experience have taken our pupils' GCSE results to levels
described as 'outstanding' by OFSTED. Mark College removes
the barriers to learning so that students can experience the full
National Curriculum.

The college is also recognised for its care. Work with students'
self-esteem and self-confidence was the subject of a recent
University study. Conclusions from this independent study have
been presented at three international conferences and we are
very proud of the findings from this research.

DCSF approved CReSTeD 'SP'
DFEE Highly Effective School Certificate 1998
Independent Schools Council Award for Excellence 1999
Ofsted 2007 top rating 'outstanding' in sports provision

**To request an information pack
or to arrange a visit please contact us:**

Please call us on: 01278 641 632
Email: markcollege@priorygroup.com
Visit: www.priorygroup.com/markcollege

PRIORY
MARK COLLEGE

Mark College, Mark, Highbridge, Somerset TA9 4NP

Unique services for unique young people

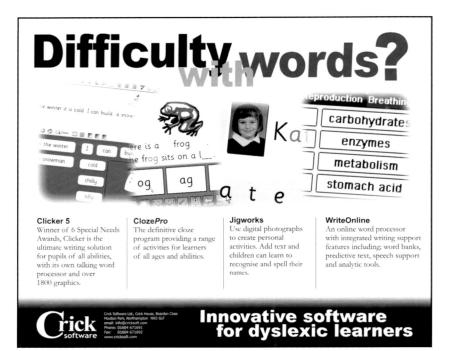

American education, programs to address dyslexia face resistance at both the system and individual level by teachers, administrators and specialists who sabotage the process of improvement for different reasons (the general failure of the recent Reading First initiative which had provided vast resources and billions of dollars is but one example in the history of American education).

So even in Texas it is still a question of which school and which classroom a child is in that determines the probability of an appropriate reading program.

Reinventing the wheel, and making it square

Although the Texas model is one that could be easily adapted to other states, in the few states where a dyslexia initiative has made it through the state legislature, a pilot program is established for that state, grants awarded, programs run for the course of the granting period; it then dies away.

The disconnect between public education and dyslexia advocacy was recently demonstrated in the State of Washington. A six year cycle of funding for special education is drawing to a close, with a funded pilot program in a handful of schools. As a pilot program (using multi-sensory programming) it was flawed from the outset by participating students being recruited if exhibiting dyslexia-like symptoms. Basically any student who had a problem with decoding was eligible, so this included English language learner students, and students with disabilities other than dyslexia. The pilot program, utilising programs like Lindamood Bell and the Wilson reading program, failed to yield the results typical of say a Lindamood Bell clinic, or an Orton-Gillingham certified program. Had the pilot program honoured the International

Dyslexia Association's definition of dyslexia:

> *"Dyslexia is a neurologically-based, often familial, disorder which interferes with the acquisition and processing of language. Varying in degrees of severity, it is manifested by difficulties in receptive and expressive language, including phonological processing, in reading, writing, spelling, handwriting, and sometimes in arithmetic"*

and if the programs were implemented with fidelity, a different outcome would have been likely.

No other state has followed Texas into legislating a solution.

In most states intervention using multi-sensory instruction and curriculum is not offered through the public schools. This has created a large industry for private providers offering tutoring.

Obviously this service is not available to all because of costs and local availability. In some states it has taken strong advocacy through state legislatures which are sympathetic to the issues of students with dyslexia to even have state departments of education acknowledge that there might be some needs that dyslexic students have which are peculiar to the disability.

Even in special education programs, where dyslexia is identified in the federal law as a recognised condition for a learning disability, schools do not take the time to determine the cause of a learning disability, only its presence. This is determined by failure to respond to instruction, or according to the definition of a Specific Learning Disability under IDEA (2004):

> *"The term 'specific learning disability' means a disorder in*

*one or more of the basic psychological processes involved
in understanding or in using language, spoken or written,
which disorder may manifest itself in the imperfect ability to
listen, think, speak, read, write, spell, or do mathematical
calculations. Such term **includes such conditions as**
perceptual disabilities, brain injury, minimal brain
dysfunction, **dyslexia,** and developmental aphasia."*

Instead of taking the next step and identifying the cause of
failure (e.g. whether the child has dyseidetic dyslexia
[characterised mainly by problems with visual processing],
dysphonetic dyslexia [characterised mainly by problems with
phonological processing], deep dyslexia, or a reading
disability not otherwise specified), schools will place students
into whatever programs they have, and these are rarely multi-
sensory.

Not all bleak

Significant changes occurred in the world of education during
the tenure of George W. Bush. This created a whole new
playing field for addressing the issue of dyslexia. The key
changes are through the No Child Left Behind legislation with
its accountability via Annual Yearly Progress (AYP), a mandate
for all children to read at grade level by grade three (8-9 years
old) and the introduction of Response to Intervention (RTI) into
schools as a means of qualifying for special education (IDEA,
2004). Education legislation has required schools to prove that
they are using a research-based curriculum which is
appropriate to the problem a student has. Furthermore, if a
school does not improve in the number of children who are
reading proficiently, they are held directly accountable. These
initiatives followed the seminal publication of the National
Reading Panel report in 2000 which highlighted the need for

intentional reading instruction, and the importance of explicit phonics instruction, among other things.

For the parent of a student with dyslexia this can offer hope. Not that the entrenched bureaucracy of public education is about to reform itself, but as an advocate the parent has a clearer path to follow in getting a school to provide services.

It will be necessary to move beyond the dyslexia label, but in the world of dyslexia research that is the trend anyway. If a child is not making progress in reading, and the parent has reason to suspect dyslexia, then the request to the school should be to address whether the reading program has successfully taught phonemic awareness. Without phonemic awareness, you can't teach phonics. If a school cannot demonstrate that the student has mastered the prerequisite skills in phonemic awareness, then the program needs to be questioned as to its effectiveness for this particular student. The demand can be made for a research-based program to be introduced. Most schools will initially utilise their core curriculum and synthetic phonics programs, and for some students this will work. When it doesn't, the parent can challenge whether those curricula are designed to be effective primarily with students of average ability, with a phonological processing disorder impacting the acquisition of reading skills. (The school cannot easily challenge the definition of phonological processing disorder, but if a parent uses the label dyslexia, then the school will talk about a medical diagnosis beyond their responsibility, etc.). Multi-sensory programs are research-based and proven to be effective for dyslexic (phonologically-disordered) students, and so eventually, unless the school is successful via some other means, the need to provide multi-sensory programming will be reached.

However, even at this point, fidelity of program implementation will become an issue. Is the program being taught properly by a trained and committed educator? At this point the parent faces the same challenge as faced by the Reading First Initiative, the multi-billion dollar federal reading initiative that overall failed to change the system. Innovative schools were successful but the majority drowned the initiative in a sea of complacency, bureaucracy and inefficiency.

A second important federal initiative is the increased emphasis on the Universal Design of Learning, uses of Adaptive Technology, and the important requirement in IDEA that before a student is removed from the general classroom for services, it must be demonstrated that accommodations and modifications are not sufficient to meet the student's needs. Current technology allows for the barriers created by dyslexia to be overcome by accommodations; while this does not meet the goal of teaching a dyslexic student how to read "normally", it does allow the student to function at their optimal cognitive level despite the dyslexia. Given the hit and miss possibilities on public schools adequately teaching dyslexic students to read, the adaptive technology approach has some real attraction.

Using adaptive technology (e.g. speech-to-text, text-to-speech, and digital books) is one aspect of Universal Design for Learning models, one aspect of accommodations required by IDEA, and one intervention strategy that might be utilized by the Response to Instruction model. Dominant in the field of adaptive technology for learning disabilities is the Don Johnston company. With a suite of tools like Read Outloud, Write Outloud, CoWriter and Draft Builder, dyslexic students can compensate for their disability. There are certainly other significant players and products in this field, such as the Clicker5 tools, Kurzweil technologies, etc., and in Britain there are companies with similar products (see, for example, E.A. Draffan's chapter in this handbook).

A recent partnership between Don Johnston and Bookshare, funded by the federal government, has made over 40 thousand texts digitally available with Read Outloud readers free to any computer a student with learning disabilities can access. Not free, but reasonably priced, the Kindle II from Amazon.com makes over 200,000 books, as well as magazines and newspapers, available digitally with text-to-speech capability. Speech-to-text software continues to improve, with Dragon Naturally Speaking still generally recognised as the leader in the field.

It is ironic that after 30 years of public schools generally failing students with dyslexia, advances in technology are now creating an educational prospect of dyslexia being seen as a learning difference rather than a learning disability. My last word must still be cautionary however, as dysfunctional public schools may be just as resistant to accepting new technology that removes the barriers for students with dyslexia as it was to providing instructional methodologies that are successful for students with dyslexia. We shall see.

Nick Hakiel is a Certified School Psychologist in Washington State.

Training for school and college staff: a quiet revolution?

Margaret Malpas

In April 2007, we faced a significant challenge. How could we further our vision to make education more dyslexia friendly? Following a bit of market research, the challenge we chose to take up was the training of parents, teaching staff and employers. This has involved astronomical amounts of work and attention to detail but is proving to be exceptionally rewarding too. After running just one day in April 2007, this year we will deliver more than 500 days of training.

Training menu

The training BDA offers is neatly summed up as being encompassed within three main areas:

- raising awareness of dyslexia
- screening for dyslexia
- offering support strategies for dyslexic individuals, their families/teachers and employers

It helps that many of our trainers are either dyslexic themselves or have brought up their own children with dyslexia. This can create a bond with parents facing the same challenges so that the trainer is able to act as a role model who has succeeded despite the difficulties, and is still smiling. This in itself can be very emotionally healing. These courses are particularly successful if we can work with parents and teachers in the same school. Within our Practical Solutions courses we show teachers how to help pupils develop coping strategies. These strategies do not stop at the school gate and parents can play a vital role in reinforcing the development of new habits and skills. If this is done as a partnership between the teacher and the parent, then the child's development in this area is accelerated and better embedded. We are also able to offer ongoing support to parents by referring them to our national helpline (which many of them use subsequently) and our local associations. We went back to parents who had been on our courses with a structured questionnaire to find out whether anything had changed after the training. All the responses were positive but some stood out. For example, in response to the question "Is there anything you have done differently since?", several parents answered "worried less."

For teachers and teaching assistants, we are able to share the latest research as we tap into a wealth of current academic work. However, one of the first things we learned was that teachers are pragmatists. They want the theory balanced with plenty of practical things they can do to make inclusive practice work well for all. With our connections with local associations we have a ready pool of coping strategies to share. We have also taken this a step further. We run courses all across England and Wales and so we have deliberately gathered tips from teachers across the regions which we then cascade to everyone. These include what to do if a child says "I'm not good at anything", to different ideas for scaffolding or differentiation.

Although, the BDA does not endorse products, the existence of our online shop means that we know what is new on the market and so we can pass on ideas about new technology and things to try. We try to demonstrate some of the software programmes but this is quite constrained by the few hours we have available. However, teaching staff can also go along to one of our regional conferences where they can see all the technology in a relaxed arena. For more practical ideas, the conference in February on 'Making Links' was particularly useful too.

Sponsoring training

Funding training is always an issue and so we have had to find innovative ways to cope with this. The fees we charge to parents do not cover our costs but make some contribution. Sometimes we are able to offer a popular programme to teachers. The income we generate there can then help us deliver a course that we really think matters to small numbers which would not otherwise be viable. One such was the course we launched in October 2008 on how to manage conditions such as dyspraxia and ADHD in the classroom. This only attracted a small number of delegates but everyone left fired up with lots of empathy with these conditions and ideas on how to manage them effectively.

Similarly, some of our team have given their time for free for some events which will encourage the development of a support team in a particular area. This was true in Calderdale recently, where we provided three training courses for parents and teaching staff using funding acquired by one of our Trustees, Jack Haymer. Following this, two of our staff have offered to do evening sessions to stimulate the growth of the local association further which will then be able to provide viable support to parents and schools in the area.

We also encourage schools to team up and we run insets for clusters which means that the per person charge is exceptionally low. In one week alone recently, we were told by no fewer than ten teachers that "this is the best Inset we have ever had". This rather makes the hard work worth it.

A very recent initiative is to offer one course per month free to a school provided they will invite in parents from other schools in the area. One school was so delighted with this that they did a fundraiser for the BDA, and another gave us a Headteacher's sticker! In Bridgend the MP, Madeleine Moon, came along to indicate her support for the work with dyslexic pupils. It is work like this that enables us to fulfil our mission and to reach people we could not otherwise attract.

Not only dyslexia...

It's no surprise to anyone that we run courses on dyslexia, but of course, with the coexistence of conditions across the spectrum of Specific Learning Difficulties, we are well placed to run courses on other less well known areas. ADHD was mentioned above but we also have modules on dyspraxia and dyscalculia. All our courses include practical things you can do. So, for instance, on our Dyscalculia Plus course, teachers go home with an entire lesson plan developed for working with children who have difficulties acquiring arithmetic skills. The latter module has proved to be increasingly popular, and with an estimated £2billion lost through poor numeracy skills in the UK, we may have one answer to the credit crunch!

Building children's self esteem

One of the things which did not prove popular sales-wise was our training in building self esteem. However, pupils will not improve their concept of themselves without self confidence. Children decide at a very early age whether school is for them or not. There is a strong link between behaviour and learning difficulties and we are regularly told by teachers in Emotional and Behavioural Difficulties units that all their pupils have some literacy difficulties. There are a number of reasons why this might occur. Some children with SpLDs respond by hiding their difficulties and trying supremely to cope. Others manifest their frustration all too obviously by playing up. The consequence is that neither group of children receives a full education. Additionally, where teachers do not respond to the child's individual learning differences, that child may not be able to learn to read or write through impairments in cognitive ability. Finally, the child who is frustrated does not motivate teachers or other adults to spend significant time with them, helping them to learn to be literate. This is known to be a key factor in development for the child with ADHD in particular. To improve literacy or numeracy, it is essential to ensure that self confidence is increased in tandem with the development of these other skills. We have, therefore, begun to include elements of self esteem training in our more general courses and especially in insets. This has proved to be very popular and interesting to delegates. We include over 50 practical tips for games and activities to develop a child's self esteem, and this is always well received.

Next steps include our overseas programmes with training already scheduled for Germany.

Accreditation

Recently we have offered accredited training more widely. Some participants are able to get funding from their school or college. However, others are prepared to fund themselves through these courses. These include individuals who desire to work with special needs pupils, or those who have become newly appointed SENCOs. We particularly applaud those who are keen to develop their skills to work with children with special educational needs.

We are, of course, very much behind the campaign to get a specialist teacher in every school. However, when you consider that there are approximately 27,000 schools in England and Wales but only 2,300 specialist teachers (members of Patoss), that's just 8% of schools reaching that target. We are training about 10,000 people per year now and they are thereby skilled to identify and support children and adults with dyslexia in schools and in workplaces. So, have we started a quiet revolution?

If you would like to find out more about our courses, then do contact us on 0845 251 9004, email paulb@bdadyslexia.org.uk, or check out dates and locations on our website at www.bdadyslexia.org.uk

Margaret Malpas is the BDA Chair of Trustees

Strategies for Success

Parents make a difference!

Valerie Muter and Helen Likierman

If you are a parent of a child with dyslexia, being informed about what dyslexia is and knowing how to build up a wide range of helping strategies will make a huge difference to how your child copes. Parents are in the unique position of being at hand to guide and support their child throughout the school years. Try this Quiz:

How much do you know about dyslexia?

Mark "True" or "False" then check your answers overleaf.

1. Dyslexia is more common among boys than girls   True or False

2. Many children who develop dyslexia have had early (pre-school) speech and language problems   True or False

3. All children with dyslexia have exceptional talents   True or False

4. Dyslexia is more common in left-handers   True or False

5. Playing games like "I Spy" with letter sounds can help young children with dyslexia   True or False

6. Children with no reading problems cannot have dyslexia   True or False

7. You can tell whether children have dyslexia from the kinds of spelling errors they make   True or False

8. Children with dyslexia are usually clumsy   True or False

Quiz Answers

1. Dyslexia is more common among boys than girls   True

2. Many children who develop dyslexia have had early   True
   (pre-school) speech and language problems

3. All children with dyslexia have exceptional talents   False

4. Dyslexia is more common in left-handers   False

5. Playing games like "I Spy" with letter sounds can   True
   help young children with dyslexia

6. Children with no reading problems cannot have   False
   dyslexia

7. You can tell whether children have dyslexia from   False
   the kinds of spelling errors they make

8. Children with dyslexia are usually clumsy   False

(but sometimes True)

Dyslexia – get the facts

Dyslexia defined: Children with dyslexia have literacy levels
that are out of keeping with their ability level and other skills.
They almost all have difficulty in processing speech sounds in
words (phonological awareness). As a result, they find it hard
to learn how to decode or 'sound out' printed words. Many
more boys than girls have dyslexia and it is known to run in
families. This means that it has a genetic basis.

How early can you tell whether your child has dyslexia? Most
parents won't notice that anything is wrong until their child
starts school and struggles to learn the alphabet and to read
simple words. However, we know that many children could be
spotted earlier. One of the first signs in some (though not all)

children who go on to have dyslexia is that they are slow to talk and sometimes have trouble understanding what others say to them. This means that children who have delayed speech should be kept a close eye on when they start school because they may well need extra help with reading – even if by the time they start school they're speaking well. Another early sign of dyslexia is lack of awareness of speech sounds in words. So there are likely to be problems remembering nursery rhymes and playing "I Spy".

Some myths about dyslexia: Many people believe that if their child is left-handed it will hamper their reading and writing skills. However, dyslexia is no more common in left-handers than in right-handers. Another myth is that all children with dyslexia have exceptional talents. Many will, and all children have relative strengths as well as weaknesses, but there is no scientific evidence that dyslexia is a "gift". It has been thought for a long time that children who reverse their letters and make funny spelling errors must have dyslexia. But the fact is children with dyslexia make the same sorts of spelling errors as younger children who are at the same spelling age level as them.

Do children with dyslexia share the same profile of difficulties? The actual problems shown will vary from one child to the next. This is because the underlying phonological processing difficulties can range from mild through to severe. As a result, some children with mild difficulties will escape reading problems but are likely to have long-standing spelling and writing problems. Also, some children learn to overcome many of their problems by compensating through their strengths. For example, children with a good vocabulary are able to use context clues in stories to help them identify words they struggle to decode as well as helping them understand the content. Finally, many children will have another specific learning difficulty on top of their dyslexia such as dyspraxia (clumsiness), attention problems, and maths difficulties; these are usually referred to as 'co-occurring problems'.

How Parents Can Help at Home

Top tips for the early years (ages 4-6)

Read story books to your child every day

This will help with many early skills that are important for reading, like:

- learning about how books work, i.e. conventions of print like titles, front and back of book, reading from left to right (sit so your child can see the print and pictures while you read)
- teaching children new words for spoken vocabulary
- building up concentration span
- increasing familiarity with printed letters and word shapes
- developing 'listening comprehension' (listening for meaning which is important to later reading comprehension)
- stimulating imagination
- promoting interest in books

Play sound games with words

These help the development of phonological awareness necessary for decoding. When playing these games the letter sounds (not the names) should be used:

- I Spy
- Yes/No rhyming games, e.g. do these words rhyme or sound the same? *bat-cat* (yes), do these words rhyme? *bag-bit* (no)

- Joining sounds together to make words, e.g. what word do these sounds make 'b-i-g'? (*big*), 's-t-i-ck' (*stick*); separate the sounds by about a second as you say them
- Taking away sounds from words (this is harder, but most 6 year olds should be able to do it), e.g. "say the word *cat*, now say *cat* without the /c/ sound" (*at*). "Say the word *meet*, now say *meet* without the /t/ sound" (*me*)

Teach and keep practising letter sounds from an early age

Use flashcards for single letters as well as alphabet books, alphabet friezes and picture story books.

Top tips for the middle years (ages 7-12)

Keep reading with your child

Importantly, have your child read out loud to you on a regular basis, every day if you can. Ten minutes a day gives your child good opportunity to:

- practise decoding (with support from you if needed)
- build up a word-specific reading vocabulary (including key words like the ones below)
- increase reading speed and fluency

Practise key word spellings

There are 100 commonplace words (like *was*, *then*, *here*, and so on) that make up half of the words we routinely read and write. If your child can learn these, his/her spelling error rate will be greatly reduced. Write these words on flashcards and post-its and practise them regularly.

Teach word identification strategies

Children with dyslexia find it very difficult to decode words, so help them get round this problem by using other clues to identify words. Encourage your child to decode an unfamiliar word as far as he/she can (even notoriously irregular words like *yacht* have some sound-to-letter consistencies, in this case the first and last letters). You can then guide your child to use story content and word context to help them "best guess" at the reading of the word – so if it's a story about sailing, when they come across a word that begins with 'y' and ends with 't', they can work out that the word is most likely to be *yacht*.

Another good strategy is to draw your child's attention to the position of the word in the sentence. One six year old boy we assessed recently, who had very poor reading skills but excellent spoken language, was able to use sentence position cues effectively. He struggled to read the sentence "I look after her little ones". He read as far as "I look" and then paused. He studied the first letter /a/ and then came up with the word 'after', a word he was completely unable to read out of context.

Note that these strategies are not a substitute for teaching phonological awareness and letter/sound identification skills but a way of making reading easier when needed. Also, when your child is reading a story to you, mostly just keep the flow going by correcting errors and instantly supplying words your child is struggling to read.

Don't forget reading comprehension

The main point of reading is 'reading for meaning'. Just reading words or sentences is 'barking at print'. Check that your child can *understand* what is being read by:

- asking him/her to tell the story back to you
- asking specific questions about the text
- asking 'inference' questions; this means asking for information that is not explicitly stated in the text, such as "how do you think that boy might feel?", "what do you think could happen next?", "can you make up a different ending to the story?"

Top tips for keeping on track

Keep homework under control

Homework can so easily become a source of struggle for the child and strife for parents. Parents can help to promote harmony and reduce conflict by:

- encouraging the 'Homework Habit' through always starting soon after returning from school or clubs; have a clear place to work and keep distractions to a minimum
- encouraging the preparation and planning of homework; know what needs to be done, how long it should take, when it is due at school, what materials are needed
- suggesting that work is done in short 'chunks' of time using a kitchen timer; work up to 15 minutes for older children before having a short break of a couple of minutes (a longer break can come after an hour of working)
- using an organisation chart; draw up columns with headings like 'date given', 'work due in by', 'work handed in on time', 'teacher's mark or comment' so that you and your child can monitor how the homework is going
- linking the organisation chart and the chunks of work time to a systematic reward scheme to reinforce good homework habits; for younger children use stickers and stars, for older

children use a points system, and use praise for all (to make these schemes really effective they need to be carefully planned, filled in daily, never linked to punishment for naughty behaviour, and rewards should come sufficiently often to be motivating)

Beat disorganisation by:

- encouraging routines for bed-time, meal-times, waking up times, as well as for homework
- teaching time-management through routines and also setting aside the right amount of time needed for homework, making sure there is time built in for leisure and enjoyment after
- creating early on the practice of organising papers and books into subjects and files
- ensuring homework and equipment for the next day are packed and ready near the front door before bed-time
- using lists for tasks to be done and ticking them off on completion
- putting reminder stickers or post-its in places where they can be seen to make sure that important tasks are not forgotten
- *always* using rewards of some kind to reinforce all the above until they become routine and automatic

Revise and pass exams by:

- listing (or getting your older child to list) the topics or syllabus to be examined
- making sure all missed work has been caught up on (check with a teacher and/or a reliable other child)
- drawing up a revision chart; tick topics off each time they are revised so there is a visual record for the child of the work he/she has done (it will also be easy to see what still

needs to be revised)

- working in small time chunks and changing topics frequently to avoid boredom and inefficient learning
- using memory aides such as post-its with notes/key words on, made-up rhymes and dictating machines to reinforce what has to be learned
- preparing for exams well in advance and using lots of repetition as both are essential for the child with dyslexia to succeed
- having the whole family do something relaxing the night before – and suggesting an early night too!

A final most important tip. Get yourself and your child into good habits and routines for practising skills and for coping well. BUT don't let your child's learning difficulties take over your or any of your children's lives. Keep a sense of perspective. Remember that your child with dyslexia can go on to do very well at school and in later life, and you will have played an important role in that process.

To find out more about your child with dyslexia, and practical tips for helping at home:

Visit our website: www.psykidz.co.uk

Read our book for parents of children aged 7-14 years: Muter, V. & Likierman, H. (2008). *Dyslexia: A Parents' Guide to Dyslexia, Dyspraxia and Other Learning Difficulties*, London: Vermilion.

For helping your pre-school child with possible dyslexia:

Likierman, H. & Muter, V. (2006). *Prepare Your Child for School*, London: Vermilion.

Likierman, H. & Muter, V. (2008). *Top Tips for Starting School*, London: Vermilion.

Dr Valerie Muter is a consultant clinical psychologist at Great Ormond St Children's Hospital. She has carried out published research in the field of early reading development and dyslexia. Dr Muter was a consultant psychologist at Dyslexia Action for 20 years, and continues to work with, and to advise on the needs of, children with dyslexia.

Dr Helen Likierman is currently working as a school counsellor in a large mixed school. She worked for many years in the NHS and was a consultant psychologist for Dyslexia Action for a number of years. She also still sees children who might have dyslexia, dyspraxia or other learning difficulties and advises parents.

Dyslexia - changing perceptions

Mike Juggins

Dyslexia in CONtext

"The point is not merely to understand the world, but to change it..." (Karl Marx)

I'm a self-taught writer, and without a spell check and the invention of cut and paste I would be stuffed. It is therefore very ironic that I attempt to explain why media other than just written words are needed if we are to move the debate on. I believe that... if we can involve more dyslexic people then we stand a better chance of positively changing how society views and then supports dyslexic people of all ages.

In truth, formal education has not been too kind to me. I struggled to achieve as a very dyslexic child in a predominantly text-based education system, and have had to witness the same for many others.

However, for the last ten years I have tried to influence policy and practice positively, and to involve many more fellow dyslexics in this process. I really welcome the opportunity to contribute to this handbook. My aim, like many others, has always been to raise greater understanding and appreciation of dyslexia.

Viewed as a gift or a curse, dyslexia is the country's biggest disABILITY. Yet for many it remains hidden, for fear of humiliation or a sign of weakness. Dyslexia affects 1 in 10 of the general population. Many people view their dyslexia as simply a natural difference in brain functioning (learning style) based on neurology, whilst others also feel that highly developed visual, spatial, and lateral thinking skills can come hand in hand with the difficulties.

Unfortunately, the medical model of disability still dominates the issue, whilst the real voices of dyslexia remain mostly on the margins. At times, it would seem that the world of dyslexia is dominated by cranky theories that relate to the causes of dyslexia, and costly remediation products or tuition in areas of difficulty.

The national dyslexia charities have done well keeping dyslexia in the public eye. However, there is a real need to involve many more dyslexics in the debate about education, support services, employment and health issues. I want the new Disability Duty slogan, that reads "nothing for us without us", to become reality.

Image and word mutually advance understanding

I feel that information and news about dyslexia, and its many complexities, need to be in visual formats such as video streaming from a web site. It is not just what gets communicated, but how we communicate, that is as important.

Put another way... a multi-media approach needs to be adopted and used across the board regarding how dyslexia, a disability that often impacts on people's literacy skills, is debated. Last year the Government made a call for evidence regarding dyslexia and education. Only a small percentage of respondents were actually dyslexic. This was almost certainly due to the text-based method of their call for submissions.

Now we all know that the world of words, in the printed format, is closed to many dyslexic people. Dyslexics experience difficulty with text-based modes of communication; therefore special emphasis needs to be placed on disseminating information in accessible formats. For example - MP3s, podcasts, web sites, videos and diagrams.

I don't think that the issue will move on as dyslexic people are not getting the information they need to make positive changes in their own lives. Information is power, and when government departments and major stakeholders produce information solely in text-based formats, it disables me and many other dyslexics.

In order to practise what I preach, there is a video version (podcast) of this ARTicle streamed at www.voicesfromthemargins.co.uk, and on the BDA website. Voices from the Margins is a small charity with the big aim of enabling people from society's margins to learn new skills, build confidence and tell their stories through the arts.

I have just heard that a new trust, The Dyslexia and SpLD Trust, has been set up with a key aim of promoting improved practice and outcomes for (and with?) individuals with dyslexia. As the Creative Director of Voices I sincerely hope that I can be of service to this trust in meeting this aim and actively involving many more dyslexics in the debate regarding positive change.

A change in the way the issue of dyslexia is communicated would, I'm sure, lead to real inclusivity and understanding, and thereafter bring about a positive revolution in the education system...

Dyslexics drowning in the mainstream

'If I hear I forget, if I see I understand, if I do I remember' relates to modern ways of looking at learning styles: Auditory, Visual and Kinesthetic. This age-old proverb gives us a key to the responsibility society has in providing equal access for all learners.

Dyslexia, from the Greek dys – meaning difficulty, and lexia – meaning words, only explains some of the difficulties we experience. Memory and organisation are also affected. However it is the negative impact of "word schools" on self-esteem that often remains into adult life.

We continue to teach and test in words despite what we know about learning styles (or should that read learning needs?). It seems so short-sighted when an individual's intellect is still often measured in relation to their literacy skills. Especially when you consider all of the wonderful innovations dyslexic minds have given the world.

Virtually every fellow dyslexic that I have ever met suffered emotional damage whilst at school. Most are so deeply concerned that future generations do NOT have to go through the same experiences as they did at school. The harsh facts are that we do not screen for dyslexia enough, and that most dyslexics still go unidentified and unsupported. Organisations like Adult Dyslexia Access, who are based in the North West, have been screening and supporting adults for ten years. Dyslexia needs to be understood by everyone entrusted with teaching or training a dyslexic thinker. Teacher training needs to take place with all teachers, not just the new ones. Limited classroom support combined with extra time during exams is simply not enough.

Accessible information motivates success

Historically, educationalists have attempted to change the way the child naturally learns rather than adapt teaching methods to match learning styles. This needs to change, and I know that most of our wonderful teachers are capable of learning the strategies necessary.

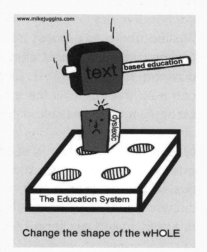

Change the shape of the wHOLE

Dyslexics do need to be taught in a way that acknowledges their weakness but, MORE importantly, focuses on their strengths. The use of multi-sensory teaching strategies would benefit most students, but especially dyslexics. Providing dyslexics with the opportunity to be fully involved in learning should be the key goal of policy makers. Facilitating an engagement in the wonder that is learning and not, as is often the case, leaving them on the periphery – a social under-class in the making.

From what I know of the 'No to Failure' and Xtraordinary People initiatives, it is clear that many like-minded people are pushing for change also. We just need to get the message out there in accessible formats. There is such a waste of potential as most dyslexics struggle.

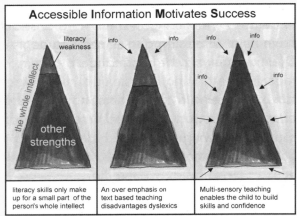

As I have said, each individual has the ability to process information in all numbers of ways; finding one's own most effective mode is vital if intellectual potential is to be fulfilled. Computers and new technologies can help students, but the emphasis must be on making the curriculum as accessible as possible.

Most of the curriculum is needlessly fragmented by professionally-defined subject areas. This does not serve the dyslexic student, or in fact many non-dyslexic students, in most circumstances, as it means that ideas and concepts that are naturally linked get separated.

We use all of our senses simultaneously when learning: seeing, smelling, hearing and feeling. When these senses are merged with insight, imagination, ambition and empathy in a relaxed and happy state, you have a potent mixture. Each brain perceiving and processing differently, each mind wonderfully powerful and yet uniquely special.

Making tasks visual or practical, and avoiding large amounts of text books, allows for real creativity and cognition on the part of the student and teacher. Using a flow chart, making a working model or running computer visualizations enables students to understand in a real and substantial way. Promoting discussion also enables students to understand and often bed-down new information.

However, being dyslexic is not just about being a poor reader or speller, it can also manifest itself in an individual's ability to order their own thoughts and ideas, particularly on paper. Short-term memory difficulties are also common... hold on! I think I have already written that.

At school, confidence is usually shattered and potential unfulfilled for dyslexics. How can it be that 50% of the prison population is dyslexic? Over- proportionate rates within unemployment, mental health and homeless figures also dictate that change is urgently needed in the way society views and deals with dyslexia.

Dyslexics of the world untie

Unidentified dyslexia is costing the country billions. Greater understanding, and thereafter support in the workplace and across the education system, must come soon, redressing the balance and enabling society to benefit from the abilities that many dyslexics have.

An identified, and thereafter supported dyslexic person can be a real asset in any workplace and learning situation. Often they bring a uniquely different way of thinking and problem solving. However, the vast majority continue to struggle in our very text- dominated society.

Well, enough words as you have the pictures that come with this article that carry their own meanings. I really do wish I could have ended this article in a more positive way...

So I will: **Dyslexia, focus on ability!**

"Those are my principles, and if you don't like them... well, I have others". (Groucho Marx)

Mike Juggins is Creative Director of Voices from the Margins. He has run creative workshops, lectured and shown inspiring films internationally on the issue of dyslexia. He is a member of the arts dyslexia trust and has produced visual material for both the BDA and Dyslexia Action over the last ten years. As an artist, Mike's first love is painting and his vibrant expressive oil paintings are rapidly gaining in reputation. For further details please visit www.mikejuggins.com.

Dyslexia – sporting preferences and achievements

David Grant

Dyslexia colours and shapes a wide range of everyday experiences and choices, including sports preferences. There is also the tantalizing possibility that being dyslexic results in enhanced sports performance. This latter statement is more contentious than the first, but both are derived from data I have collected when carrying out diagnostic assessments for specific learning differences, over a nine-year period.

I have a personal reason for being interested in sporting achievement and dyslexia, as one of my sons is dyslexic and was county 800 metres champion for three consecutive years. There is also a professional reason. As there is a high degree of commonality between dyslexia and dyspraxia, and about a third of the individuals I see are dyspraxic or have signs of dyspraxia, it is vital to distinguish between these two specific learning differences.

In order to do so it is necessary to determine whether there is a history of clumsiness and/or motor coordination difficulties, for these are the defining characteristics of dyspraxia. Therefore, wherever I carry out a diagnostic assessment I collect information about an individual's motor coordination history. This includes asking questions about sporting preferences and achievements.

It is not surprising that many dyslexic readers, but not all, say they looked forward to taking part in sports at school as it is a practical activity and not an academic one. That is, it is a lesson free of reading and writing requirements. However, on looking back over the life histories of individuals I had diagnosed, I was very surprised by just how many reported a history of high level sporting achievement. On average, one in every eight or nine dyslexic individuals (i.e. approximately 12%) I have seen over the past nine years had reached a county or national standard, with almost equal numbers of males and females. Of the 100+ individuals who had done so, approximately 15% had achieved at a national level.

Defining sporting achievement

The question of how to define a high level of sporting achievement is open to interpretation. For some individuals, just being selected to be a member of a netball or football B-team is cause for celebration. However, I have used a more objective measure, that of whether an individual has been selected to represent their county or country, or has achieved a high placing in a national event by receiving a bronze, silver or gold medal.

To be selected to represent your county (e.g. Middlesex) means that, for your age group and in your chosen event, whether it be the long-jump, 100 metres, tennis or netball, you are the best – or in the case of a team – one of the best in your county. This then results in opportunities to represent your county at regional events, such as the South-East England Championships, as well as national events, such as the National Schools Championships. Intuitively, you might expect dyslexic children to do particularly well at sports given that, for some at least, sports represent an escape from the classroom.

However, there is a difference between enjoying an activity and excelling at it. Practice and enthusiasm alone do not guarantee success, for I have seen many individuals who, in spite of enthusiasm and total commitment to their sport, do not manage to reach a county or national level. There must therefore, also be underlying physiological factors to achieving sporting excellence.

The role of the cerebellum

In spite of the outstanding achievements by dyslexic sportsmen such as the UK's Steve Redgrave, Jackie Stewart and Duncan Goodhew, and US Olympic heroes Bruce Jenner (Gold, decathlon) and Greg Louganis (double Gold, diving), there is very little research on dyslexia and sporting achievements. What there is suggests that those with dyslexia will not perform as well at sports as those without dyslexia. For example, Angela Fawcett and Roderick Nicolson (2001), state:

> *"we argue it is difficult for dyslexic children to become expert in any skill, whether cognitive or motor. Consequently, they will suffer problems in fluency for any skill that should become automatic via extensive practice"* (p. 92).

In principle, their argument is a simple one. They claim that the part of the brain known as the cerebellum plays a vital role in skill development, irrespective of whether the skill is a motor or cognitive one and, in the case of dyslexic readers, the cerebellum does not function as well as it might otherwise do. That is, there is cerebellar dysfunction, which results in a lack of automaticity when learning a wide range of skills.

It is true that the cerebellum is linked with motor movement, and it plays an important role in integrating sensory information, but I find it difficult to accept the validity of

Fawcett and Nicolson's hypothesis that dyslexic readers have problems with acquiring motor skills for a very simple reason – I have met too many dyslexic children and adults who are extremely good at sports. These include a world sailing champion, a winner of the Young Horse Middle East Eventing Competition, a member of the GB Olympic Cycling Time Trial team, a gold medal winner of the Scandinavian Singles Ice Skating competition, winners of bronze medals at a Wu Shu (martial arts) World Open event, and the floor event in gymnastics in a national competition in Chile.

Why it is important to establish whether dyspraxia is present

All these sports require considerable motor skills, including balance. The question then becomes one of why is there such a mismatch between the proposition that dyslexia is a reflection of cerebellar dysfunction, and the number of dyslexic individuals I have seen who have very good, if not exceptional, motor skills? Waugh and Sherrill (2004) help provide an answer, for they point out that researchers in general have not always taken sufficient care to distinguish between dyslexia and dyspraxia – the key defining features of dyspraxia being clumsiness and difficulties with motor coordination.

A number of surveys have shown that dyspraxia occurs with about the same frequency as dyslexia – that is, in about 1 in 20 people. In my experience about 10% of the dyslexic individuals I see are both dyslexic and dyspraxic, while about another 15% have signs of dyspraxia. In addition, approximately 25% of dyspraxic individuals show some signs of dyslexia. It will therefore be the case that, unless very specific steps are taken by researchers to differentiate clearly between dyslexia and dyspraxia when selecting participants for a research project, it is inevitable that dyspraxia will also be present to a greater or lesser extent in any group selected on the basis of being dyslexic. This is why, when Ramus et al (2003) did take care over their screening process, they reported motor difficulties for just 25% of their dyslexic participants. That is, motor difficulty per se is not a defining characteristic of dyslexia.

The brain – a computer model

What we can be much more certain about is that the typical dyslexic reader will perform much more strongly on tests of verbal and visual reasoning and understanding than on tests of working memory (i.e. short-term auditory memory) and processing speed (speed of visual scanning and copying). The analogy I use to help individuals understand this imbalance is to suggest that they think of their brain as being rather like a computer. It is as if their word-processing software and graphics chip are good (often excellent), but they are short of RAM and have a slow processing chip. This configuration results in it taking longer to process information, and a need to work using smaller chunks to avoid crashing memory. It is, however, important to note that there are sometimes significant variations to this profile since dyslexia takes different forms.

A number of dyslexic individuals I have seen said that although they enjoy taking part in sports, they are not keen on team sports. I suspect a key factor underlying this lack of enthusiasm is the need to multi-task in team sports. For example, you need simultaneously to remember the coach's instructions, take account of what team mates are telling you, and remember the rules of the game - often complex ones about which space you can and cannot occupy. In other words, you need a lot of

RAM. On the other hand, sports such as running are less complex and so being able to remember is not as important.

The relationship between sport preference and cognitive profile

When I looked at the sports in which dyslexic readers have achieved county level, for girls the individual sports of cross-country, athletic track events and swimming were dominant, comfortably ahead of hockey and netball. For boys the picture was slightly more complicated, with rugby being the dominant sport, followed by athletic track events, badminton, cross-country and swimming. However, when I looked at the profile of male rugby players and male runners (track and cross-country), the rugby players, on average, had much higher scores on working memory tests than did the runners, whereas the runners had higher scores on tests of processing speed than did the rugby players. In other words, there was a noticeable tendency for cognitive profile to be reflected in the sport chosen. Whilst this kind of analysis could not be undertaken for those who had achieved at a national level, because the numbers were too small, with one exception all were engaged in individual sports rather than strategic team sports such as football, basketball, hockey or netball.

The need to think seriously about the impact of dyslexia on sports training is well illustrated by a rugby player I saw who mentioned having difficulties with remembering pre-arranged line-out codes[1]. He was big, could jump well, and had good ball-handing skills. However, his ability to remember what to do when a line-out code was called out was so poor that his team captain took to standing behind him to tell him when to jump.

1 A line-out is where the rugby ball is thrown into play from the touchline and the two teams compete to see who can catch the ball.

A number of individuals have told me that when they began learning a team sport they forgot rules more frequently than their team mates and, as a consequence, were picked on by members of their own team. This resulted in a loss of enthusiasm. Just as in an academic setting, PE teachers and coaches need to adopt teaching and training techniques that are suited to the learning style of dyslexic individuals. It should be realised that what might be an initial slowness in learning, and even forgetfulness such as not bringing the right kit to school, is often part and parcel of being dyslexic. However, it is my experience that an active participation in sport is, for many dyslexic children and adults, an important learning experience in that it helps to develop and strengthen their skills of organisation and time management. For some, it is also an essential part of enhancing self-esteem.

References

Fawcett, A.J. & Nicolson, R.I. (2001). Dyslexia: the role of the cerebellum. In A. Fawcett (Ed.), *Dyslexia: Theory and Good Practice*. London: Whurr Publishers.

Ramus, F., Rosen, S., Dakin, S.C., Day, B.L., Castellote, J.M, White, S. & Frith, U. (2003). Theories of developmental dyslexia: insights from a multiple case study of dyslexic adults. *Brain, 126*, 841-865.

Waugh, L.M. & Sherrill, C. (2004). Dyslexia – implications for physical educators and coaches. *Palaestra* (on-line journal), January 22.

Further reading

Grant, D. (2008). Sporting preferences and achievements of dyslexic and dyspraxic sports men and women: Lessons for London 2012? *Dyslexia Review, 20*, 1, 31-37.

Dr David Grant is a Chartered Psychologist and writer who specialises in diagnostic assessments for adults with specific learning differences.

Legislation

What is the Special Educational Needs (Information) Act?

Sharon Hodgson, MP

The Special Educational Needs (Information) Act (www.opsi.gov.uk/acts/acts2008/ukpga_20080011_en_1) went through Parliament during 2008. The Act amends the 1996 Education Act to give the Secretary of State two additional powers: the power to collect more information about children with Special Educational Needs, including dyslexia, and to publish annually information which will help to improve outcomes for children with Special Educational Needs (SEN). In this chapter I want to explain how the Bill came about and what it will mean for children with dyslexia as well as examining what more can be done to keep up pressure in Parliament for better support in schools for dyslexic pupils.

There was a time when anyone campaigning for better education for children with dyslexia would have been accused of talking 'mumbo jumbo'. Not any more.

As a parent with a severely dyslexic son I know only too well the pressure and frustration many other parents in similar situations face. I know how difficult it can be to take on the system in an attempt to get the best for your child. Sometimes it can feel like the hoops you have to jump through will never end.

The government has made huge increases in the financial support available to local authorities for SEN. There have been developments in one-to-one learning which will make a real impact on the education of our children, but dyslexic pupils need extra help and support. All of our brains work in different ways and although there are proven teaching methods which work well for the majority, we have to ensure that the minority are equally well supported.

The SEN (Information) Act was designed to place a spotlight on the lack of information about support for children with SEN in our schools. We all know that there is a 'patchwork quilt' of provision but without accurate monitoring we cannot hope to establish best practice.

The passage through Parliament

Once the Bill was tabled it became clear that there was a great degree of support from across all of the political parties. We managed to secure support from a number of high profile MPs including the former Education Secretary David Blunkett MP, Chairman of the Children Schools and Families Select Committee Barry Sheerman MP, and the author of the Government's review into Speech, Language, and Communication needs John Bercow MP.

The passage of the Act meant that MPs and Peers had the chance to speak out about their own experiences of dyslexia. Some talked of their own difficulties with dyslexia and others spoke of the impact of dyslexia on children known to them. The Conservative MP Christopher Fraser emphasised the explicit link between unidentified dyslexia and poor literacy, long-term failure at school and limited employment opportunities. The Labour MP for Swindon, Anne Snelgrove, highlighted the need for better recognition of dyslexia in local authorities and teacher training institutions. She reflected that in order to achieve this it was necessary to tackle the parts of the educational system where the reality of dyslexia was still denied.

In the House of Lords the Liberal Democrat peer Lord Addington spoke eloquently of the problems he faces with his dyslexia, and remarked that one of the strengths of the bill would be in enabling campaigners to discover what does not work as well as what does work.

The opportunity to debate dyslexia and other Special Educational Needs in Parliament has been vital to raising awareness amongst politicians of the challenges we still face in making sure that dyslexia is recognised in our schools, and that pupils with dyslexia are properly supported.

How the Bill will affect children with dyslexia

The provisions of the Bill cover all children identified as having SEN. The Department for Children, Schools and Families (DCSF) has identified a number of key themes which need to be addressed when the Bill is implemented. These are:

- wellbeing, including perceptions of personal safety and emotional and physical health
- early identification and intervention to enhance future life chances
- progress and narrowing attainment gaps, wherever possible
- commissioning services, based on robust analysis of need and evaluation of performance
- integrating data on outcomes for children and young people

These themes are reinforced by proposals to:

- clarify the role of schools in promoting the well-being of their pupils
- streamline monitoring, inspection and reporting

arrangements for schools and local authority services for children

It is good to see these factors spelt out so clearly for consideration. We all know the impact which dyslexia can have on a child's wellbeing. Too often children struggling with dyslexia are labelled naughty or disruptive which can quickly lead to problems in the playground and the home. I even heard one example of a dyslexic child who kept being given lines as a punishment for failing to remember sports or classroom equipment; this shows quite clearly how a lack of understanding on the part of teaching staff can have a negative impact on the wellbeing of the child. After all, you wouldn't ask a physically disabled child to run laps of a running track as a punishment.

Intervening early in a child's life when something is causing added difficulty is vitally important in helping them to fulfil their potential. At the end of 2007, the Government announced a £2.5 million pilot scheme to help children who have dyslexia, identified through the 'Every Child a Reader' programme. Half the children will receive additional one-to-one 'Reading Recovery' support and the other half will receive one-to-one tuition from specialist dyslexia teachers. Reading improvement will be closely monitored. If specialist provision demonstrates significant impact, ministers will look at how assessment and specialist dyslexia support could be rolled out nationwide as best practice. The pilot scheme will provide intensive support for children in some schools in 10 local authority areas.

Using the data already published by the Department, it is clear that there is a gap between progress and attainment for those children with SEN such as dyslexia and the more mainstream rates of progress and attainment. Closing this gap wherever possible is essential and monitoring outcomes will be vital in raising expectations for children with dyslexia.

It is difficult to argue for better provision of services when we cannot accurately identify all children with dyslexia and other SEN. That is why I am particularly pleased that the DCSF will consult to develop consistent national standards for School Action, School Action Plus and Statements of Special Educational Need. At the moment, type of need is only recorded for children who are considered to require School Action Plus levels of support or statements. Given that of the 1.9 million children with SEN, 1.6 million children are at School Action level, this means that 1.6 million children in this country are identified as having a Special Educational Need such as dyslexia but there is no record of what their actual need is.

That is why I was so pleased that we were able to pressure Ministers into agreeing to a review of the national criteria for identifying a child's primary need. At the moment there are a few very broad categories into which children are placed. There are a whole host of organisations, including the British Dyslexia Association, who want to see specific categories for specific needs. One of the major problems with taking such an approach is that very often children have more than one need which makes recording primary needs difficult. It is important to keep making the case that only by knowing exactly how many children have specific needs in our schools can we ensure full and proper provision to enable them to reach their full potential. In order to try and improve the ability of teachers to identify and support children with dyslexia, Ministers have undertaken to review the effectiveness of ongoing professional development courses for teachers as part of the Bercow

Review. There will also be a new Masters degree for teachers which will contain specific modules on supporting children with SEN such as dyslexia.

All of the new information which is collected and will be published as a result of the SEN (Information) Act will be published annually starting from this September. At first it will be published through existing outlets such as the DCSF website but I am hopeful that we will be able to move towards a system which will see the publication of a report card for Local Authorities. This will enable parents to monitor performance and scrutinise where there may be room for further improvement.

Many of the changes in how information is collected and published are little technical tweaks but their impact over time should be much greater. In 2009/10 OFSTED are undertaking an investigation into SEN in schools, and parts of their review will focus on issues which were raised during the passage of the SEN (Information) Act.

Where next for dyslexia in Parliament?

The changes secured thanks to the SEN (Information) Act are all positive steps in the right direction but there remains plenty more work to be done. In order for all of these changes to have the maximum impact we must continue to press for improvements in teacher training.

We must train one teacher in every school to become a qualified dyslexia specialist. This does not mean recruiting new staff but encouraging existing staff to broaden their skills. A qualified specialist in every school would be able to provide support to other teachers. They could also develop a school-specific long term strategy for dealing with dyslexia.

We must also ensure that all newly trained teachers are able to spot the signs of learning difficulties such as dyslexia. All too often children's problems are swept under the carpet by both parents and teachers. By ensuring that all teachers are trained to spot such problems we can make sure that direct help and support is available for future generations.

Some of the great inventors, innovators and entrepreneurs in the history of our country were dyslexic. These include Winston Churchill, Albert Einstein, Richard Branson, John Lennon and Andy Warhol.

Indeed Winston Churchill once said:

"I was on the whole, considerably discouraged by my school days. It was not pleasant to feel oneself so completely outclassed and left behind at the beginning of the race."

We should not be leaving anybody behind in 21st century Britain. If we are going to remain a force to be reckoned with in a global economy we need to make the most of everybody's talents. Anyone who tells you otherwise is talking mumbo jumbo.

Thanks to the work of the British Dyslexia Association and other dyslexia charities, we have a strong lobby in Parliament. There is support on all sides of the house for increasing awareness of dyslexia in our schools and workplaces and I am confident that in 2009 and beyond we can keep securing a brighter future for children with dyslexia.

Sharon Hodgson is Labour MP for Gateshead East and Washington West. When Sharon's SEN (Information) Bill received Royal Ascent in July 2008, Sharon became only the fourth female MP this decade to steer a private member's bill successfully through Parliament.

Navigating the tribunal procedure: from beginning to SEND

Lindy Springett

History of parental appeals

Prior to the early nineties, the only ultimate avenue open to parents[1] who felt their child wasn't getting the help in school that they desperately needed, was an appeal to the Secretary of State for Education. This was generally agreed to be a rather unsatisfying and unrewarding process.

In 1994 news came of a new appeal procedure, alongside a Code of Practice for Special Educational Provision in schools. For the first time, there was to be a truly independent body to hear parents' appeals against decisions made by Local Education Authorities in England about their child's education. The Special Education Needs Tribunal (SENT) quickly proved to be a very effective system. Parents and Local Education Authorities both sent their paperwork into the Tribunal office and ultimately attended a Hearing (unless the case was settled prior to this). A legally qualified Chair presided, with two Specialist Members who had Local Education Authority experience and/or Special Education Needs experience.

The Hearing was as informal as possible and really was very parent-friendly. In 2002, the Disability Discrimination Act was widened to include educational settings, and accordingly the Tribunal's remit was widened to include disability appeals too. It was thus renamed The Special Education Needs and Disability Tribunal (SENDIST).

1 Please take all mention of 'parents' to mean 'parents/carers'

The Tribunal becomes part of a new structure

Now there has been more change, which has proved a little confusing at first. From 3rd November 2008, SENDIST ceased to exist as a stand-alone body, and came under the auspices of the Ministry of Justice. It became part of a new two-tier Tribunal structure, the First-tier Tribunal and the Upper Tribunal. The two new Tribunals consist of Chambers that group together jurisdictions dealing with similar work, or requiring similar skills.

Special Educational Needs and Disability was put into the Health, Education and Social Care (HESC) Chamber of the First-Tier Tribunal. Appeals against the tribunal panel's decisions, which previously went to the High Court, now go to the Upper Tribunal.

The official name for this Tribunal became "First Tier Tribunal Health, Education and Social Care Chamber (SEN & Disability)". It was promptly decided to reduce this far from catchy name to a mere "SEND"!

By becoming part of a larger Tribunal, the structure of SEND had to change somewhat to comply with general Tribunal procedures. But the people who run SEND were determined that the philosophy would not change and the best practices of the old system would be preserved. Particularly that it would remain as parent-friendly and informal as humanly possible and unswervingly focused on the best interests of the child.

The Tribunal Chairs will now be known as Tribunal Judges, but this title will be used as little as possible, as it does sound intimidating for parents. They are exactly the same people who were previously the 'Chairs' and are not Judges in the legal sense of the word. The Specialist Members are now called

'Non-Legal Members', but again are exactly the same people as before.

Case management

The most noticeable change, as far as parents and Local Authorities are concerned, is the introduction of a Case Management system at an early stage in the proceedings. Case Management is designed:

- to ensure that everyone has as much evidence as possible as early as possible. Parents will now see the Authority's reasons for their decisions at week six or seven, rather than having to wait to see them in the bundle of Tribunal papers received approximately two weeks before the Hearing
- to help both parents and Local Authorities to prepare their cases
- to help the Tribunal to reach appropriate decisions in the interests of the child, that are based on full information to help both parents and Local Authorities to identify the issues as early as possible, so they may be able to reach a settlement and avoid the need for a Hearing

Approximately 50% of the appeals that are sent in are straightforward. In these cases, the parents will receive:

- an acknowledgement of their appeal
- an "Automatic directions" form. This gives information about the Hearing. It also asks for any missing paperwork, and gives the date to send it back by
- a form to send back to the Tribunal with information on witnesses, representatives, special needs, etc.

More complicated cases will be looked at by a Tribunal Judge who has been selected to participate in Case Management. Parents will then receive:

- an acknowledgement of their appeal
- a Further Information Form, giving the provisional date of a Final Hearing and asking for information regarding
- areas of disagreement in the case
- any new written information to be provided in support of the case
- dates of appointments that have been made with independent professionals
- witnesses, supporters and a representative, if appropriate
- whether the child will be attending the Hearing
- any special needs of attendees who may require adjustments at the Hearing

Their case will then subsequently result in:

- a three-way telephone Case Management conference with the Case Manager, parents and Local Authority, or
- a face-to-face three-way Case Management conference, or
- continued communication on paper

After a Case Management Conference (either by telephone or face-to-face), the parents and the Local Authority will be sent a form detailing the outcomes. This will include a list of additional evidence that is to be sent in (such as Education Plans, Attendance records, etc). A Case Management Conference will NOT be a chance to put cases and points of view forward. It is merely to sort out what extra information the Tribunal needs, and to ensure that everyone is complying with requests for information and deadlines. It should be of great help to many parents, giving them guidance as to what information will be useful to their case.

The timetable will now look like this:

Parents must appeal within two months of the decision being *sent* to them by the Local Authority (they could previously appeal within two months of *receiving* the decision). They should send in as much of their evidence as possible at this stage. Then,

Week 0	The appeal is registered and forms are sent out to parents and Local Authorities
Week 6/7	Local Authorities send their response to both Tribunal and parents
Week 8/9	Further information forms are sent back to the Tribunal
Week 10	Case Management conferences (if necessary)
Week 16	Final deadline for submission of evidence
Week 17	Bundles are received by parents and Local Authorities
Week 18	Working documents are finalised and sent
Week 20	The Hearing takes place

It is hoped and expected that Local Authorities will work with parents at least to start to come to an agreement over provision for their children. To this end, they are encouraged to produce a 'working document' showing the areas of agreement and disagreement reached so far.

There is also a "Request for Directions" form that parents and Local Authorities can use at any stage of the process to request a variety of things, such as extension of time, submission of additional evidence, postponement etc. Such requests will also be considered by a Case Manager.

Other changes

The other main changes to the system are:

- participants at a Hearing can be required to give their evidence under oath
- the Tribunal now has to give permission for a case to be withdrawn before the Hearing, thus ensuring that the outcome *is* exactly what the parents have understood it to be
- expert Witnesses' written evidence should incorporate a paragraph to say that they are truly independent and conscious of their duty to the Tribunal, rather than to either party
- formerly the number of witnesses was restricted to two. To comply with human rights, there will now be no restriction, but a request will have to be put in to have more than three witnesses
- Local Authorities can request an order to allow them to assess a child. However, this will only be granted where they can put forward an excellent case. Where there are sound reasons for parents' refusal, the Tribunal is exceedingly unlikely to make an order
- similarly, parents can request an order to allow a professional of their choosing to go into school to make an assessment on their child
- the Local Authority has to obtain the views of the child *concerning the issues raised by the proceedings* (rather than just the child's general views on all matters). Otherwise, they have to give good reasons why these views cannot be obtained
- non-speaking observers and supporters can be allowed into the Hearing, at the Tribunal's discretion

The future

It is confidently expected that Case Management of future Tribunal cases will effect real change for parents and children. It is already resulting in cases being settled far earlier. This will also produce savings. For example, over a two month period last year, cases withdrawn at the last moment or not being ready for the Hearing on the day cost £60,000.

The Tribunal Administration Office in London was closed shortly before the changes occurred. All administration was transferred to the existing office in Darlington. Obviously this was not ideal, and resulted in a greatly increased workload at just the wrong moment. The office has now caught up with itself again and returned things to an even keel. Unfortunately, though, there are plans probably to transfer all the administration from Darlington to Loughborough in 2010.

These new procedures and the timetable will be reviewed in six months' time and any desirable adjustments should be put into place after September 2009. As much feedback about the new system as possible is requested by the Tribunal Office, both as to what is working well and if there are any pitfalls.

There are also several more events that may change things yet again:

- there is a possibility that permanent exclusion appeals may be heard by SEND;
- "Enabling Consent" will be abolished in September 2009. This is the procedure of getting the Secretary of State's approval for a child with a statement to go to an independent school, or special school which does not have the prior approval of the Department for Children, Schools and Families;

- there is a forthcoming OFSTED review on all aspects of Special Educational Needs, which may ultimately affect the way SEND operates. The results of this review are not expected for at least 18 months to two years;
- currently, an appeal to SEND cannot be in a child's name, but must be in the parent's name. This is being changed in Wales, and the English Parliament is considering whether it will follow suit.

In spite of all the changes, the Tribunal remains an impartial and parent-friendly system, and panels will unfailingly continue in their endeavour to achieve the best outcome for each and every child. Parents and advisors have learnt to trust the Tribunal, and there is no reason why their trust should not continue to be justified in the future.

Contact details for SEND:

Website: www.sendist.co.uk
Email:sendistqueries@tribunals.gsi.gov.uk

Special Educational Needs & Disability Tribunal, 2nd Floor Old Hall, Mowden Hall, Staindrop Road, Darlington, DL3 9BG.

Special Educational Needs helpline: 0870 241 2555
Discrimination helpline: 0870 241 2555

NB The tribunal details in this article were correct at the time of going to press.

Lindy Springett is Vice Chair of the Dyslexia Association of Bexley Bromley Greenwich & Lewisham. She has been a BDA Befriender (parental advocate) for 15 years and was a trustee of the BDA for six years

Biological Factors in Dyslexia

Genetic and environmental factors in dyslexia

Emma Hayiou-Thomas

Introduction

We've known for more than a hundred years that dyslexia runs in families. The chances are that if you have dyslexia, someone else in your family does too: maybe a sibling, cousin, parent, or grandparent, though it might not have been recognised or diagnosed (they might have been described as 'not very good readers', or even just 'struggling in school'). The fact that dyslexia runs in families gives us a good starting point for figuring out the causes of dyslexia: are genetic or environmental factors responsible for reading difficulties? The complication is that families share both their genes and their environments, and we need a way to untangle these two factors.

Twin method

Luckily, nature has provided a perfect experimental set-up for teasing apart the genetic and environmental factors that cause differences in people's behaviour and cognitive skills, including reading. Identical twins are effectively clones of each other, as they share 100% of their DNA. Non-identical, or fraternal twins, share 50% of the DNA that varies from person to person (bear in mind that all humans share 99.9% of their DNA – only 0.1% is different from one person to another, and it is this tiny fraction that underlies inherited differences in behaviour – including differences in reading skill). However, apart from the amount of DNA they share with their co-twins, identical and fraternal twins are the same: they are exactly the same age, grow up in the same house, with the same parents and siblings. This can help us get at the causes of dyslexia in the following way:

Step 1: find a large group of twins with dyslexia
Step 2: see whether their co-twins also have dyslexia (or at least, are struggling with reading)
Step 3: see if more identical co-twins than fraternal co-twins have dyslexia

If so, it must mean that genes play a role in causing dyslexia, because that's the only 'extra similarity' that identical twins have compared to fraternal twins: their extra genetic similarity is driving the extra similarity in reading.

Heritability of dyslexia

Twin studies of dyslexia have found exactly the pattern described above: the co-twins of identical twins with dyslexia are more likely also to have difficulty with reading than are the co-twins of fraternal twins with dyslexia. Two separate large-scale studies, one in the UK and one in the USA, have reported that 50%-70% of the difference in reading between groups of children with dyslexia and the rest of the population is due to genes. A similar amount of genetic influence, or heritability, has been found for reading ability in general. This suggests that there aren't any special genes for dyslexia, but that the same genes are responsible for both good and poor reading: if you have one version – or allele – it will help your reading, and if you have a different version, it will hinder reading. However, the only way to know whether this is really the case is to find the actual genes involved.

Finding the genes for reading and dyslexia

Finding the genes that influence reading and dyslexia is a difficult task, because as with most complex behaviours, it is likely that there are very many genes involved, each of them playing a small part in the overall process. It is also important to bear in mind that, although it's convenient to refer to 'reading genes' or 'dyslexia genes', there is actually no such thing. Genes just give instructions for making proteins, which make up cells, which build hearts and livers and brains, which, among other things, learn to read. Unsurprisingly, given the many complicated steps between genes and a behaviour like reading, any genes that do influence reading are almost certain to influence other things also, some of them completely unrelated to reading.

Nevertheless, in the last few years there has been an impressive amount of research in molecular genetics hunting for the genes that account for variation in reading skill. At least nine chromosomal regions, or loci, have been found to be linked to dyslexia, and of these, there have so far been three chromosomes on which specific genes have been identified: Chromosomes 3 (gene *ROBO1*), 6 (genes *KIAA0319* and *DCDC2*) and 15 (gene *DYX1C1*). All four of these genes seem to be involved in brain development, and particularly in the way that neurons move to the appropriate part of the brain very early in life. A recent study focusing on gene *KIAA0319* found that it was associated not only with dyslexia, but with reading ability in the general population too.

Environments influencing reading and dyslexia

It is clear that genetic factors play an important role in reading and dyslexia. However, the heritability estimates referred to above are considerably less than 100%: if 50-70% of the variation in reading is due to genes, it must mean that 30-50% is due to environmental factors. Since the 1970s, it's been known that children in poorer socioeconomic circumstances are more likely to have difficulties with reading. This is partly because many (but not all!) disadvantaged families do not have a good home literacy environment, which is one of the most important environmental factors for reading that we know about. Children's reading tends to thrive in homes where there are a lot of books, and with parents who present a positive attitude toward education and reading, who present reading as an enjoyable and entertaining activity, and who read with their children from an early age. The language environment is also an important factor, since oral language skills are a foundation for reading. Parents who encourage their children to talk, and who use rich and varied vocabularies in conversation with their children, are helping to promote strong language skills, which in turn help reading. Factors outside the home, such as the school a child attends and the teaching methods used, can also make a big difference.

Gene-environment interplay

Genes and environments do not act in isolation, but instead work together throughout a person's life. One of the ways this can happen is through what's known as a gene-environment correlation (rGE). This means that people's genes can influence the kind of environment they experience, which in turn can influence their behaviour. For example, some dyslexic parents might avoid reading with their children, and not buy many books, because they themselves do not find reading enjoyable. These parents will pass on both their 'dyslexia genes' and a poor home literacy environment to their children, so that both the genes and the environment driven by those genes, would be putting the children at higher risk of dyslexia. This type of situation is called a 'passive gene-environment correlation'. An alternative scenario is one where dyslexic children themselves, rather than their parents, affect the reading environment: because the children find reading difficult, they might avoid reading books (an 'active gene-environment correlation'), or they might encourage their parents to do other activities with them instead of reading (an 'evocative gene-environment correlation'). In all these cases, the 'dyslexia genes' in the family are contributing to a poorer reading environment for the children, including less practice with reading, and practice is fundamentally important for fluent reading, as it is for most skills. There is some research evidence that both passive and active gene-environment correlations may play a role in reading development, in the way described above. However, we will soon be able to test these possibilities much more thoroughly, using some of the actual genes identified for reading.

A second way in which genes and environments work together is in what's known as a gene-environment interaction (GxE). In this case, it's not that the genes shape the environment (as happens in rGE), but that a person's response to the environment depends on his or her genes. For example, we might think of a given teaching method as an environmental factor relevant for reading: it may be that people respond more or less well to this teaching method depending on the particular versions of 'reading genes' that they have. Currently there is no research that has looked at this directly, but again, it will soon be possible to test this possibility using identified genes.

Finally, it is important to point out that because genes and

The Unicorn School

An independent co-educational day school for pupils with dyslexia from 6-13 years

- ➢ Daily intensive 1:1 specialist tuition for <u>all</u> pupils

- ➢ A family atmosphere committed to raising pupils' confidence and self-esteem

- ➢ Class sizes of ten to ensure individual attention and for the child, easy access to their teacher

- ➢ CReSTed "Sp" Status for whole school provision

- ➢ Dyslexia trained, dedicated teaching staff at the cutting edge of dyslexia, dyspraxia and dyscalculia through regular inset opportunities

- ➢ National Curriculum followed with mornings devoted to literacy and numeracy

- ➢ Touch-typing tuition as part of IT curriculum

- ➢ A wide range of sporting activities

- ➢ Celebration of the talents and strengths in sports, art, music, IT, CDT and drama which so often go hand in hand with dyslexia

- ➢ Minibus transport available

For a warm welcome
come and visit us at
The Unicorn School
20 Marcham Road
Abingdon OX14 1AA

info@unicorndyslexia.co.uk
www.unicorndyslexia.co.uk
Tel/ 01235 530222

AFTER THE UNICORN?
We aim to return our pupils into 'dyslexia friendly' mainstream independent and state schools as soon as they have the literacy skills, confidence and strategies to feel that they can succeed. On average pupils are with us for two years.

environments constantly interact, there is no such thing as genetic determinism. Even in cases where genes appear to be the dominant force, changing the environment in the right way can 'overpower' the genetic effect. One dramatic example of this is PKU, or phenylketonuria, a genetic disorder in which the body can't metabolise a particular amino acid. Left unchecked, this can result in serious learning disability. However, a simple change in the environment – leaving this amino acid out of the baby's diet – prevents these problems. Less dramatically in the case of dyslexia, even though genetic factors appear to be important, there are many teaching methods that work very well in helping to improve reading, as many dyslexic readers, their parents and teachers already know!

Genes for reading... and language

Oral language is an important foundation for learning to read, and there is a lot of evidence showing that phonology – how words sound – is especially important for reading. Children who can easily pick out that 'cat' and 'mat' rhyme with each other, or that 'cat' and 'coat' start with the same sound, find it relatively easy to break words apart into their separate sounds and map these onto letters; this is one of the key processes in learning to read. Likewise, children who find this type of task difficult are very likely to have difficulties in learning to read.

Research from twin studies has shown that phonology, like reading, is highly heritable: it is strongly influenced by genetic factors. It also turns out that there is a large amount of genetic overlap between reading and phonology: many of the same genes are important for both of these skills. It may be that at least some of the 'reading genes' are actually 'phonology genes', and that it is through phonology that they affect reading.

Although phonology is the most important part of language underpinning reading, other language skills – such as vocabulary and grammar – also play a role, particularly for reading comprehension. Genes do influence these language skills, but less so than for phonology. Instead, environmental factors, like the ones discussed earlier, seem to be more important for developing the parts of language that are concerned with what words mean, and how we put them together in a meaningful way. These environments, together with the genetic factors that affect language, then go on to influence reading.

In summary, oral language skills – and particularly phonology – are important foundations for reading, and they share much of their underlying aetiology, whether genetic or environmental, with reading. There are then additional genetic factors that are specific to reading.

Conclusion

Reading is a complex skill, so it is not surprising that the underlying causes are also complex. Genes seem to play a very important role in accounting for differences between people in how well they learn to read. Environmental factors also play an important role, though it seems to be a smaller role than that of genes, at least in the countries where most of this research has taken place (mainly the UK, USA and Australia). Although it is still early days, good progress has already been made in identifying some of the many genes that are important for reading and dyslexia, and for the foundational language skills underpinning reading. These findings are exciting in themselves, and will also make it possible to look at how genes work with the environment as children learn to read. This will be immensely helpful in choosing and designing teaching methods that are tailored to individual children's needs.

References and further reading

Books on behavioural genetics, which include some discussion of reading and dyslexia:

Plomin, R., DeFries, J.C., McClearn, G.E., & McGuffin, P. (2008). *Behavioral Genetics 5th Edition*. New York: Worth Publishers.

Rutter, M. (2006). *Genes and Behavior: Nature-Nurture Interplay Explained*. Oxford: Blackwell Publishing.

Journal articles and chapters on the topics discussed in the chapter:

Byrne, B., Olson, R.K., Samuelsson, S., Wadsworth, S., Corley, R., DeFries, J.C., & Willcutt, E. (2006).Genetic and Environmental Influences on Early Literacy. *Journal of Research in Reading, 29, 33-49.*

Gayan,J., & Olson,R.K. (2001). Genetic and environmental influences on orthographic and phonological skills in children with reading disabilities. *Developmental Neuropsychology, 20, 483-507.*

Harlaar, N., Spinath, F. M., Dale, P. S., & Plomin, R. (2005). Genetic influences on word recognition abilities and disabilities: A study of 7 year old twins. *Journal of Child Psychology and Psychiatry, 46, 373-384.*

Hayiou-Thomas, M.E. (2008). Genetic and environmental influences on early speech, language and literacy development. *Journal of Communication Disorders, 41, 397–408.*

Hayiou-Thomas, M.E., Harlaar, N., Dale, P.S. & Plomin, R. (in press). Preschool speech and language skills and reading at 7, 9 and 10 years: aetiology of the relationship. *Journal of Speech, Language & Hearing Research.*

Paracchini, S., Scerri, T., & Monaco, A.P. (2007). The genetic lexicon of dyslexia. *Annual Review of Genomics and Human Genetics, 57-79.*

Pennington, B. F., & Olson, R.K. (2005). Genetics of dyslexia. In M. Snowling & C. Hulme (Eds.), *The science of reading: A handbook* (pp. 453-472). Oxford: Blackwell Publishing.

Petrill, S.A., Deater-Deckard, K., Schatschneider, C., & Davis, C. (2005) Measured environmental influences on early reading: evidence from an adoption study. *Scientific Studies of Reading, 9, 237-259.*

Dr Emma Hayiou-Thomas is at the Centre for Reading and Language at the University of York

Dyslexia from a cognitive neuroscience perspective: making links and moving forward

Joel B. Talcott and Emma E. Birkett

The 7th International Conference of the BDA was held in the spring of 2008 under the theme, 'Making Links: From Theory to Practice'. This theme could not have been more appropriate and timely because it outlined at least two crucial agenda items for dyslexia research moving forward through the next decade. The first showcases the importance of fostering an increased understanding of dyslexia as a syndrome with multiple dimensions, including those that overlap substantially with other developmental difficulties. The second encapsulates the need to improve the way information between research and practice is communicated. The topic of this brief review focuses primarily on the first of these objectives, with the inclusion of this chapter in the BDA handbook hopefully helping to move us forward by at least some small degree on the latter.

Normal and atypical reading development from a cognitive neuroscience perspective

Cognitive neuroscience is a research area that is inherently interdisciplinary, integrating such apparently disparate areas as psychology, neuroscience, genetics, computer science and biology in an effort to understand the neural basis of complex human behaviours such as reading. The benefit for understanding dyslexia is that each of these perspectives offers a different toolkit which can be used to test hypotheses at different levels of analysis. For example, we are now able to probe the causal path of specific reading difficulty from genetic risk, through intervening neural mechanisms, to ultimately describing both normal and atypical reading development as observed in the clinic and in the classroom. Of particular relevance to a cognitive neuroscience perspective of dyslexia is describing not only how reading is implemented by the brain, but also determining the relevance of other features of dyslexia that extend beyond literacy, especially those that are shared with other developmental disorders. For example, given that subtle deficits of motor control are sometimes found in dyslexia (Nicolson, Fawcett, & Dean, 2001), we can now focus on how these deficits are related to reading. We can also investigate the reasons why highly prevalent developmental disorders, such as dyslexia, developmental coordination disorder and attention deficit hyperactivity disorder (ADHD) are all associated with motor difficulties (Rochelle & Talcott, 2006) and often co-occur in the same children.

From genes to reading, via the brain

From an evolutionary perspective, reading is a very new human activity. It then follows that reading relies upon the recruitment of brain areas that are not specific to literacy-based activities, and that the genes that effect reading skill are also not specific. With these principles in mind, we briefly examine some of the current knowledge about genetic and neurological influences on reading and dyslexia, and follow-on with some ideas about the importance for understanding co-morbidity in this context.

Neuroimaging studies have identified a cortical network which provides a template for reading (Fiez & Petersen, 1998; Demonet, Taylor & Chaix, 2004; Turkeltaub et al., 2002). In people with dyslexia there is evidence for reduced neural activation within the regions that comprise this network, and importantly, lowered correlations between the activity of these areas during the performance of reading tasks (Paulesu, et al., 1996; Pugh, et al. 2000). The degree of this functional coordination is likely paramount to skilled reading development and may provide a neural signature for both reading skill and for literacy difficulties (Pugh, et al., 2000; Shaywitz, et al., 1998). There is also some evidence that appropriate training may help to 'normalise' the pattern of activity within the reading network in children with dyslexia (Temple et al, 2003). Current research is focussing on the nature of functional connectivity (Deutsch, et al., 2005; Niogi & McCandliss, 2006), including the genetic and environmental influences involved and how they are manifest in the brain throughout development. As it turns out, improved understanding of connectivity as it pertains to reading may also shed light on the nature of the co-morbidity between dyslexia and other developmental disorders.

Nowhere has progress in understanding dyslexia been advancing more rapidly than in the description of its genetic basis. Although it has long been known that reading disability tends to aggregate in families (e.g. Thomas, 1905), such familial clustering alone does not provide definitive evidence for a heritable basis. The reason for this is that families can differ substantially in their environments as well as in their genetics, for example in the extent to which literacy activities are practised and reinforced in the home. However, by comparing samples of identical and fraternal twins, the heritability of reading skills can be directly estimated; different types of twins are raised in largely equivalent environments but their genetic similarity is systematically different. Twin studies have helped to demonstrate that approximately half of the variability in reading skill in the population is attributable to genetic factors (DeFries & Gillis, 1993). These findings alone should resolve the debate about whether dyslexia is a myth.

Multiple genes contribute to dyslexia risk, with the strongest evidence pointing to several independent regions on separate chromosomes (Williams & O'Donovan, 2006; see also the chapter by Hayiou-Thomas in this handbook). Importantly, the genes implicated in dyslexia are generally the same as those associated with literacy skills within the normal range (Paracchini, et al., 2008). This reinforces the idea that reading differences between good and poor readers can be best modelled in terms of quantitative differences rather than qualitative ones. Several dyslexia risk genes are involved in the process by which early development of the brain is regulated (e.g. Paracchini, et al., 2006). Alterations in the functioning of these genes may result in atypical development of the neural architecture that supports reading. Advances in non-invasive neuroimaging techniques now allow us to evaluate and track such neural development in children (Rumsey & Ernst, 2009). This will eventually yield data on the normal time-courses and developmental trajectories associated with both normal and atypical reading development.

Shared mechanisms in learning difficulties: the generalist genes hypothesis

Recent reviews have revealed some very interesting findings about the genetic basis of developmental disorders, including dyslexia. In particular, many of the genetic effects linked to common learning difficulties overlap significantly, which suggests that they are general, rather than specific in function (Plomin & Kovas, 2005). Further study of the functions of these 'generalist genes' may ultimately help us better understand not only the aetiology of normal and atypical reading development, but also the common denominators of risk that might explain why different learning difficulties overlap so frequently.

So how might generalist genes work? As an example, one of the (many) genetic associations found in dyslexia is on chromosome 6, and specifically with a particular gene, KIAA-03019 (KIA) (Paracchini, Scerri & Monaco, 2007). KIA is functionally involved in early brain development and helps to mould the development of the cerebral cortex by promoting the process of cell migration in the pre-natal brain (Paracchini et al, 2006). The activity of this gene may be reduced in dyslexia, resulting in anomalous migration of neurons during development; evidence that is consistent with a range of neurological data obtained from persons with dyslexia (e.g., Galaburda & Kemper, 1979; Siliani, et al., 2005). Importantly, KIA has not only been implicated in dyslexia, but also influences reading ability across the range of skill in the overall population (Paracchini et al., 2008). Such a gene thereby fulfils one of the main criteria of the generalist gene hypothesis (Plomin & Kovas, 2005), namely that the genetic effects will explain normal variation in skills as well as being associated with dyslexia.

To better understand how such genetic risk factors manifest in behaviour depends on the identification of 'endophenotypes'. In the context of developmental difficulties, these are underlying neural mechanisms that are intermediate between the behavioural and genetic layers of explanation. Given the evidence already presented, structural and functional connectivity would appear to be one potential endophenotype worthy of further investigation in dyslexia. However, connectivity differences are also implicated across a range of other developmental disorders with a heritable basis (e.g., Belmonte, et al., 2004). Better understanding of the nature and sources of variability in such neurological features may ultimately provide the context to explain why so many children fit the profile of more than one diagnostic category.

Summary: making links

Co-morbidity refers to the presence of more than one diagnosis occurring in an individual at the same time. In the context of developmental disorders such as dyslexia, co-morbidity often refers to the necessity of having more than one diagnosis to account for all the symptoms present in any individual. Many common developmental disorders, such as dyslexia, ADHD, language impairment and coordination disorder, co-occur much more frequently than would be expected from their prevalence rates in the population (Pennington, 2009). In fact it is becoming widely accepted that pure cases of, for example, dyslexia are the exception rather than the rule (e.g. Karmiloff-Smith, 2006). A recent study of 100 children attending a clinic in the US reported not a single case of a 'pure' developmental disorder (Pauc, 2005). However, in light of the evidence briefly reviewed above, the high degree of overlap between disorders might not really be that surprising after all.

Making links therefore pushes us away from studying categorical deficits in isolation, and toward the development of more comprehensive and multi-dimensional theories of learning disorders (Pennington, 2006; Rubinsten & Henik, 2009). Therefore, paradoxically, to improve understanding of developmental disorders, researchers and practitioners need to move away from single-deficit definitions (Gilger & Kaplan, 2001), and instead take into consideration children's profiles of strengths and weaknesses across a broader range of cognitive and behavioural continua. Given that dyslexia is one of the most visible and well-studied of the developmental disorders, our success in this endeavour will impact significantly upon how other disorders are conceptualised and the way in which diagnosis and interventions are ultimately approached.

References

Belmonte, M.K., Allen, G., Beckel-Mitchener, A., Boulanger, L.M., Carper, R.A., & Webb, S.J. (2004). Autism and Abnormal Development of Brain Connectivity. *The Journal of Neuroscience, 24,* 9228-9231

DeFries, J.C. & Gillis, J.J. (1993). Genetics and reading disability. In: R. Plomin and G. E. McClearn (Eds.). *Nature, nurture, and psychology (pp. 121–145).* Washington, DC: American Psychological Association.

Demonet, J.F., Taylor, M.J., & Chaix,Y. (2004). Developmental dyslexia. *Lancet, 363,* 1451-1460.

Deutsch, G.K., Dougherty, R.F., Bammer, R., Siok, W.T., Gabrieli, J.D.E., & Wandell, B. (2005). Children's reading performance is correlated with white matter structure measured by diffusion tensor imaging. *Cortex, 41,* 354-363.

Fiez, J., & Petersen, S. (1998). Neuroimaging studies of word reading. *Proceedings of the National Academy of Sciences (USA), 95,* 914-921.

Galaburda, A.M., & Kemper, T.L. (1979). Cytoarchitectonic abnormalities in developmental dyslexia: a case study. *Annals of Neurology, 6,* 94-100.

Gilger, J.W., & Kaplan, B.J. (2001). Atypical brain development: a conceptual framework for understanding developmental disabilities. *Developmental*

Neuropsychology, 20, 465–481.

Karmiloff-Smith, A. (2006). The tortuous route from genes to behaviour: A neuroconstructivist approach. *Cognitive, Affective and Behavioural Neuroscience, 6, 9-17.*

Nicolson, R.I., Fawcett, A.J, & Dean, P. (2001). Developmental dyslexia: the cerebellar deficit hypothesis. *Trends in Neurosciences, 24,* 508-511.

Niogi, S.N., & McCandliss, B. D. (2006). Left lateralized white matter microstructure accounts for individual differences in reading ability and disability. *Neuropsychologia, 44,* 2178-2188.

Paracchini, S., Scerri, T., & Monaco, A.P., (2007). The genetic lexicon of dyslexia. *Annual Review of Genomics and Human Genetics, 8,* 57-79.

Paracchini, S., Steer, C.D., Buckingham, L.L., Morris, A.P., Ring, S., Scerri, T., Stein, J., Pembrey, M.E., Ragoussis, J., Golding, J., & Monaco, A.P. (2008). Association of the KIAA0319 dyslexia susceptibility gene with reading skills in the general population. *American Journal of Psychiatry, 165,* 1576-84.

Paracchini, S., Thomas, A., Castro, S., Lai, C., Paramasivam, M., Wang., Keating, B.J., Taylor, J.M., Hacking, D.F., Scerri, T., Francks, C., Richardson, A.J., Wade-Martins, R., Stein, J.F., Knight, J.C., Copp, A.J., LoTurco, J., & Monaco, A.P. (2006). The chromosome 6p22 haplotype associated with dyslexia reduces the expression of KIAA0319, a novel gene involved in neuronal migration. *Human Molecular Genetics, 15,* 1659-1666.

Pauc, R. (2005). Comorbidity of dyslexia, dyspraxia, ADD, ADHD, OCD and Tourette's syndrome in children: A prospective epidemiological study. *Clinical Chiropractic, 8,* 189-198.

Paulesu, E., Frith, U., Snowling, M., Gallagher, A., Morton, J., Frackowiak, R.S.J., & Frith, C.D. (1996). Is developmental dyslexia a disconnection syndrome? Evidence from PET scanning. *Brain, 119*, 143-157.

Pennington, B.F. (2006). From single to multiple deficit models of developmental disorders. *Cognition, 101, 388-413.*

Pennington, B.F. (2009). *Diagnosing learning disorders: a neuropsychological framework (2nd. ed).* New York: The Guilford Press.

Plomin, R. & Kovas, Y. (2005). Generalist genes and learning disabilities. *Psychological Bulletin, 131*, 592-617.

Pugh, K.R., Mencl, E., Shaywitz, B.A., Shaywitz, S.E., Fulbright, R.K., Skudlarski, P., Constable, R.T., Marchione, K., Jenner, A. R., Shankweiler, D. P., Katz, L., Fletcher, J., Lacadie, C., & Gore, J.C. (2000). The angular gyrus in developmental dyslexia: Task-specific differences in functional connectivity in posterior cortex. *Psychological Science, 11*, 51-56.

Rochelle, K.S.H & Talcott, J.B. (2006). Impaired balance in developmental dyslexia: a meta-analysis of the contending evidence. *Journal of Child Psychology and Psychiatry, 77*, 1159-1166.

Rubinsten, O. & Henik, A. (2009). Developmental Dyscalculia: heterogeneity might not mean different mechanisms. *Trends in Cognitive Sciences, 13*, 92-99.

Rumsey, J., & Ernst, M. (2009). *Neuroimaging in developmental clinical neuroscience.* Cambridge: Cambridge University Press.

Shaywitz, S.E, Shaywitz, B.A., Pugh, K., Fulbright, R., Constable, R.T., Mencl, W.E., Shankweiler, D., Liberman, A.M., Skudlarski, P., Fletcher, J., Katz, L., Marchione, K.E., Lacadie, C., Gatenby, C., & Gore, J. (1998). Functional disruption in the brain for reading in dyslexia. *Proceedings of the National Academy of Science, USA, 95*, 2636-2641.

Siliani, G., Frith, U., Demonet, J., Fazio, F., Perani, D., Price,

C., Frith, C., & Paulesu, E. (2005). Brain abnormalities underlying altered activation in dyslexia: a voxel based morphometry study. *Brain, 128*, 2453-2461.

Temple, E., Deutsch, G.K., Poldrack, R.A., Miller, S.L., Tallal, P., Merzenich, M.M. & Gabrieli, J.D.E. (2003). Neural deficits in children with dyslexia ameliorated by behavioral remediation: Evidence from functional MRI. *Proceedings of the National Academy of Sciences (USA), 100*, 2860-2865.

Thomas, C. J. (1905). Congenital word blindness and its treatment. *Ophthalmoscope, 3*, 380.

Turkeltaub, P.E., Eden, G.F., Jones, K.M., & Zeffiro, T.A. (2002). Meta-analysis of the functional neuroanatomy of single-word reading: Method and validation. *NeuroImage, 16*, 765-780.

Willliams, J. & O'Donovan, M. (2006). The genetics of developmental dyslexia. *European Journal of Human Genetics, 14*, 681-689.

Dr Joel Talcott and **Emma Birkett** work in the School of Life and Health Sciences, Aston University, Birmingham, B4 7ET

Neuroimaging studies of dyslexia: The hopes and limitations

Cathy J. Price and Fiona M. Richardson

Summary

In this review we consider whether sophisticated brain scanners can be used to diagnose the cause or identify the hallmarks of developmental reading difficulties. An increasing number of studies have found evidence for differences in the brain structure of good and poor readers. However, to date, these have only been observed when data are averaged over groups of participants and the results are not consistent across individuals. We argue that this is because dyslexia is not homogeneous and that further studies are required to look at how brain structure varies across subtypes of dyslexia. We also emphasise that further work is required to determine whether the observed differences in brain structure are the cause or consequence of dyslexia. We conclude with optimism that structural brain imaging will play an increasingly important role in understanding dyslexia.

Introduction

Can a brain scan diagnose developmental difficulties in learning to read? We know that reading involves the translation of visual symbols into meaning and speech sounds, and that this undoubtedly occurs in the brain. We also know that adults who were skilled readers but later suffer brain damage (e.g. due to a stroke) can acquire "dyslexia" and lose the ability to read normally, even though their speaking and intellectual abilities remain intact. Therefore it follows that some children may have difficulties learning to read because some parts of their brain are not functioning as well as others. Yet, even with the most modern and sophisticated brain scanners, it is currently impossible to see how the brain of an individual with a developmental reading difficulty differs from the brains of those who are good readers. However, there are an increasing number of studies searching for the "neural hallmarks of developmental dyslexia". In this chapter, we will summarise present findings, discuss limitations in the interpretation of these results, and end with the hope that we are one step closer to understanding dyslexia. We begin with a brief overview of what skilled reading entails and how this system is thought to break down in developmental dyslexia.

Skilled reading

Reading refers to the ability to access the language system from visual words. Cognitive modelsDivide the ability to read into at least three different components:

(a) orthographic processing of visual letter strings

(b) phonological processing that links orthographic input to speech sounds

(c) semantic processing that links orthographic input to meaning

Depending on the model, each component can be further subdivided. For example, skilled readers can pronounce

(i) new and unfamiliar letter strings (e.g. SHAP) that depend on recognising familiar letter combinations and sounding the

Cantor and Nissel offers

CHROMAGEN

A range of coloured spectacle lenses (also available in contact lens form) that has been proven to help dyslexia, as well as managing colour vision deficiency.

Further information can be found on www.dyslexia-help.co.uk

These lenses are available from around 100 registered optical practices in the UK.

 Cantor and Nissel Ltd
Market Place
Brackley
Northants
NN13 7NN

 +44 (0)1280 702002

 +44 (0)1280 703003

 info@cantor-nissel.co.uk

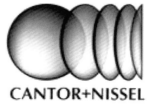
CANTOR+NISSEL

word out using their knowledge of spelling-to-sound relationships, and

(ii) familiar words with irregular spellings (e.g. CHOIR) that require whole word recognition because their spelling does not correspond to the expected sounds

The dissociation between the ability to read unfamiliar words and irregularly spelled words is particularly obvious in patients who have *acquired dyslexia* following brain damage: Some patients can read nonwords (made up words) better than irregularly spelled real words (these patients have 'surface dyslexia') while other patients show the opposite pattern (these patients have 'phonological dyslexia'). This suggests that different brain regions support different types of reading.

Difficulties learning to read

Those diagnosed with *developmental dyslexia* have difficulties with accurate and/or fluent word recognition, spelling, learning spelling-to-sound correspondences and pronouncing heard nonwords, despite an absence of any non-verbal cognitive impairment and normal educational opportunities to learn. The disorder is predominantly associated with difficulties in phonological processing, which include poor phonological awareness (ability to access and manipulate speech sounds), slow lexical retrieval, and poor verbal short-term memory. These difficulties can continue into adolescence and adulthood. Nevertheless, developmental dyslexia is not a homogeneous condition and individuals vary in their profile of linguistic difficulties. Non-linguistic difficulties, which include poor balance, co-ordination and fine motor skills also vary (Fawcett & Nicolson, 1995; Ramus et al., 2003).

Multiple theories of dyslexia are described in the literature (for further description see Ramus, et al., 2003). However, in spite of these different interpretations as to the underlying cause, dyslexia is most frequently described in terms of a deficit in accessing and manipulating the sounds of words (phonological processing). Other potential causes include:

- a deficit in the auditory perception of rapidly varying acoustic information (Tallal, 1993)
- a double-deficit in phonological processing and processes underlying rapid temporal processing (Wolf & Bowers, 1999)
- a deficit in multisensory temporal processing (Habib, 2000)
- cerebellar dysfunction affecting motor skills and thus also speech articulation (Nicolson et al, 2001)
- a deficit in visual processing pathways, which has an adverse effect on learning to read, or magnocellular abnormalities of the visual pathway to auditory and tactile modalities (Stein & Walsh et al., 1997).

These theories can be used to predict the brain regions that may not have developed normally. In addition, investigations of dyslexic brains carried out post-mortem have led to the prediction that structural brain imaging will reveal differences in the temporal lobes and visual processing areas (Galaburda et al.,1985; Livingstone et al., 1991). However, in this chapter, we take a step back from such predictions, and ask: Is there any evidence for structural differences in the brains of good and poor readers that are consistent across groups and observed in whole brain analyses?

Methods for studying brain structure using MRI

The brain images used in the papers included in this chapter were collected using magnetic resonance imaging (MRI). This technique provides high resolution images that distinguish the signal in thousands of different regions that are referred to as voxels. Voxels are the three dimensional equivalent of pixels and are typically collected with a volume of less than 2mm^3 in structural MRI protocols.

The analysis of structural MRI images typically involves the regional comparison of brain structure in two groups of participants (e.g. good vs. poor readers) or the correlation of local brain structure with language abilities. Both approaches help to localise brain regions that support language function. The most prominent techniques used in structural MRI studies of dyslexia are Voxel-Based Morphometry (VBM) and Diffusion Tensor Imaging (DTI).

VBM is conducted on a voxel-by-voxel basis using a mass-univariate analysis of the whole brain. VBM is an unbiased and objective technique as it does not rely on *a priori* regions of interest or the manual parcellation of cortical regions. In contrast, DTI uses the principles of water diffusion to track white matter pathways as water molecules diffuse along a path of least resistance, travelling in parallel to white matter fibres.

Results

To our knowledge, there are currently nine published VBM studies of dyslexia (Brambati et al., 2004; Brown et al., 2001; Eckert et al., 2005; Hoeft et al., 2007; Kronbichler et al., 2008; Pernet et al., 2009; Silani et al., 2005; Steinbrink et al., 2008; Vinckenbosch et al 2005). Eight studies reported less grey matter in group comparisons of dyslexic readers and good readers. However, the most notable features that emerge across these studies are that:

(i)   structural abnormalities are widely distributed across the brain in both hemispheres
(ii) there is a great deal of variability in the results of different studies
(iii) the results are not highly significant within each study

Despite the inconsistency, it is still possible to extract some emergent features. The most frequently reported brain regions to show structural differences between dyslexic and non-dyslexic readers are located in posterior temporal/temporo-parietal regions associated with phonological processing (Brambati et al., 2004; Hoeft et al., 2007; Silani et al., 2005; Steinbrink et al., 2008), occipito-temporal regions associated with the early stages of word recognition (Brambati et al., 2004; Eckert et al., 2005; Kronbichler et al., 2008), and the cerebellum which is typically associated with the control of motor function (Brambati et al., 2004; Brown et al., 2001; Eckert et al., 2005; Kronbichler et al., 2008). In addition, studies of white matter connections have reported group differences in a left temporo-parietal region that links speech comprehension and production regions (Silani et al., 2005; Steinbrink et al., 2008). Figure 1 shows the locations and names of the brain lobes and regions.
An alternative approach is to correlate brain structure with reading accuracy or speed, but again many regions have been identified where grey matter is highest in those who have faster reading responses (Kronbichler et al., 2008; Silani et al., 2005; Pernet et al., 2009). The lack of consistency between these VBM studies is difficult to interpret because

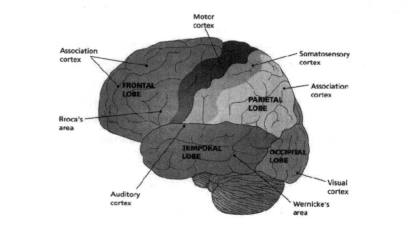

Figure 1

there were no direct comparisons of the ability to read different word types (e.g. unfamiliar words and words with atypical spellings). However, correlations of reading ability with white matter have been more consistent across studies. For instance, DTI measures of left temporo-parietal white matter have been consistently and positively correlated with faster or more accurate reading (e.g. Steinbrink et al., 2008). Nevertheless, because these positive correlations were observed in both good and dyslexic readers, they cannot be a hallmark of the dyslexic brain. Instead, they highlight the importance of left temporo-parietal white matter tracts for skilled and efficient reading.

Discussion

The study of brain structure in developmental dyslexia has been carried out on the premise that deviations in typical morphology may provide potential neural markers for poor reading, which may also give some indication as to the underlying cause/s of dyslexia. The identification of regional brain differences can provide a predictive basis for identifying children at risk of developing the disorder, as well as suggesting more effective strategies for remediation. However, there are currently two major limitations that apply to the interpretation of the results. One is that we do not know whether the differences are the cause or consequence of poor reading ability. The other is that the results are inconsistent across studies. We will discuss each of these limitations in turn.

Limitation 1: Cause or consequence

One interpretation of structural brain differences between good and poor readers is that increased brain tissue reflects increased neural resources that are a necessary precursor to learning, facilitating the acquisition of a given skill. However, there is an alternative explanation because recent studies have demonstrated that the brain changes within an individual as they learn to perform a task such as juggling (Draganski et al., 2004). Therefore, increased brain structure in good readers may be a consequence of more reading experience. Distinguishing between cause and consequence can only be established through the use of longitudinal studies. There is a need for such studies in developmental dyslexia to determine whether improvements in reading are caused by increases in grey matter within the same individuals, or whether some individuals have higher grey matter in some brain regions which enables them to attain higher levels of reading proficiency.

Limitation 2: Inconsistencies

The second limitation is that, with very few exceptions, results across studies have been remarkably inconsistent, and there is certainly no demonstration of any structural brain differences that are consistent across individuals. We think the explanation lies in the many different ways that the development of reading skills can break down. Thus, as discussed in the introduction, group differences between dyslexic and skilled readers could arise at multiple levels depending on the individuals tested. Indeed, there is increasing evidence that the ability to learn to read can be impaired in different ways (e.g. Manis et al., 1996; Zabell & Everatt, 2002). Future studies of brain structure in dyslexic readers may therefore need to focus on distinguishing neural markers for different subtypes of dyslexia.

Conclusions

Although it is difficult to interpret the results of current neuroimaging studies of dyslexia, there is optimism that differences in the brains of dyslexic and good readers may in future provide a more accurate basis for diagnosis and effective remediation. Moreover, investigating the pattern of these structural differences over time in relation to improvements in linguistic skills may provide an insight into brain regions supporting the process of compensation, which in turn may also influence remediation strategies and identify the most appropriate period for intervention.

References

Brown, W.E., Eliez, V., Menon, J. M., Rumsey, C. D., White, B.A., & Reiss, A.L. (2001). Preliminary evidence of widespread morphological variations of the brain in dyslexia. *Neurology, 56,* 781-783

Draganski, B., Gaser, C., Busch, V., Schuierer, G., Bogdahn, U., & May, A. (2004). Neuroplasticity: changes in grey matter induced by training. *Nature, 427,* 311-312

Eckert, M.A., Leonard, C.M., Wilke, M., Eckert, M., Richards,

T., & Richards, A., et al. (2005). Anatomical signatures of dyslexia in children: unique information from manual and voxel based morphometry brain measures. *Cortex, 41,* 304-315

Fawcett, A. J., & Nicolson, R. I. (1995). Persistent deficits in motor skill of children with dyslexia. *Journal of Motor Behavior, 27,* 235-240

Galaburda, A.M., Sherman, G.F., Rosen, G.D., Aboitiz, F., & Geshwind, N. (1985). Developmental dyslexia: four consecutive patients with cortical abnormalities. *Annals of Neurology, 18,* 222-233

Gaser, C., & Schlaug, G. (2003). Brain structures differ between musicians and non-musicians. *Journal of Neuroscience, 23,* 21-24

Habib, M. (2000). The neurological basis of developmental dyslexia an overview and working hypothesis. *Brain, 123,* 2373-2399

Hoeft, F., Meyler, A., Hernandez, A., Juel, C., Taylor-Hill, H., & Martindale, J.L., et al. (2007). Functional and morphometric brain dissociation between dyslexia and reading ability. *Proceedings of the National Academy of Sciences, 4,* 4234-4239

Kronbichler, M,. Wimmer, H., Saffen, W., Hutzler, F., Mair, A., & Ladurner, G. (2008). Developmental dyslexia: grey matter abnormalities in the occipitotemporal cortex. *Human Brain Mapping, 29,* 613-625

Livingstone, M.S., Rosen, G.D., Drislane, F.W., & Galaburda, A.M. (1991). Physiological and anatomical evidence for a magnocellular defect in developmental defect. *Proceedings of the National Academy of Sciences, USA, 88, 7943-7947*

Manis, F.R., Seidenberg, M.S., Doi, L.M., McBride-Chang, C., & Petersen, A. (1996). On the bases of two subtypes of developmental dyslexia. *Cognition, 58,* 157-95

Nicolson, R.I., Fawcett, A.J., & Dean, P. (2001). Developmental dyslexia: the cerebellar deficit hypothesis. *Trends in Neurosciences, 24*, 508-511

Pernet, C., Andersson, J., Paulesu, E., & Démonet, J.F. (2009). When all hypotheses are right: a multifocal account of dyslexia. *Human Brain Mapping, Feb 23; 30*, 2278-2292 [Epub ahead of print]

Ramus, F. (2004). Neurobiology of dyslexia: a reinterpretation of the data. *Trends in Neurosciences, 27*, 721-726

Ramus, F., Rosen, S., Dakin, S.C., Day, B.L., Castelotte, J.M., White, S., & Frith, U. (2003). Theories of developmental dyslexia: insights from a multiple case study of dyslexic adults. *Brain, 126*, 841-865

Silani, G., Frith, U., Démonet, J.-F., Fazio, F., Perani, D., & Price, C., et al. (2005). Brain abnormalities underlying altered activation in dyslexia: a voxel based morphometry study. *Brain, 128*, 2453-2461

Stein, J., & Walsh, V. (1997). To see but not to read: the magnocellular theory of dyslexia. *Trends in Neurosciences, 20*, 147-152

Steinbrink, C., Vogt, K., Kastrup, A., Müller, H.-P., Juengling, F.D., Kassubek, J., & Rieker, A. (2008). The contribution of white and grey matter differences to developmental dyslexia: insights from DTI and VBM at 3.0T. *Neuropsychologia, 46*, 3170-3178

Tallal, P., Miller, S., & Fitch, R.H. (1993). Neurobiological basis of speech: a case for the pre-eminence of temporal processing. *Annals of the New York Academy of Sciences, 682*, 27-47

Vinckenbosch, E., Robichon, F., & Eliez, Z. (2005). Grey matter alteration in dyslexia: converging evidence from volumetric and voxel-by-voxel MRI analyses. *Neuropsychologia, 43*, 324-331

Wolf, M., & Bowers, P.G. (1999). The double-deficit

hypothesis for developmental dyslexias. *Journal of Educational Psychology, 91,* 415-438

Zabell, C., & Everatt, J. (2002) Surface and phonological subtypes of adult developmental dyslexia. *Dyslexia, 8,*160-77.

Professor Cathy Price and **Dr Fiona Richardson** are at the Wellcome Trust Centre for Neuroimaging, University College London

Dyslexia, Creativity and the Arts

Drawing and dyslexia: some recent research

Qona Rankin and Howard Riley

The authors' experiences of art schools, particularly through the teaching of drawing and the supporting of dyslexic students, has made us think about how drawing skills could be made more accessible to students who report dissatisfaction with their drawing abilities. This is often despite them having been exposed to drawing instruction for up to four years at art school (one year Foundation Studies plus three years BA). A film made by Qona Rankin, of art students talking about their specific difficulties with drawing and their worries about how their professional practice could be detrimentally affected by their lack of skill in this area, caught the attention of Professor Alan Cummings, Pro Rector of the Royal College of Art (RCA), who was responsible for establishing a dyslexia support unit at the RCA. The film prompted him to invite Professor Christopher Kennard from Imperial College to watch it, and he gave us some practical advice as to how to engage the attention of other academics with expertise relevant to this area of research. This resulted in exploratory discussions with researchers from the RCA, Swansea Metropolitan University (SMU), Imperial College, City University, King's College, Essex University, University College London (UCL) and Middlesex University (MU). The initial meetings identified the following questions:

1. Is there a genuine link between dyslexia and enhanced ability in art and design, or is the prevalence of dyslexia among artists and designers a consequence of the failure to do well in the sciences and humanities during their early education?
2. How is functionality affected in dyslexic art students beyond

the well understood difficulties with text, for example in short term memory or the ability to organise data?
3. In particular, is there a previously unrecognised and unexplored link between dyslexia, visual and spatial sensibility in general, and the ability to draw?

These questions have not all been answered yet, but discussions generated an ongoing collaborative research project between the two present authors, Dr Nicola Brunswick of MU, and Professor Chris McManus of UCL; this collaboration has yielded some interesting insights. We have demonstrated, first of all, the potential of such a cross-disciplinary approach to exploring the relations between personality factors, perceptual problems, visual memory and drawing skills in art students who report difficulties producing accurate drawn representations of their observational experiences.

Initial findings revealed that dyslexic art students were more likely than non-dyslexic art students to have one or both parents who are artists. Other results indicate that dyslexia seems not to relate significantly to drawing ability, at least as indexed by: grades in GCSE and A level art; self-rated ability in a range of skills related to art and design (see figure 1); or interest in different areas of art and design (see figure 2).

The reason overall that so many art students are dyslexic still requires explanation, but it does seem unlikely that people with dyslexia have either special skills for drawing, or particular problems with making visual representations of the world.

While drawing ability did not relate to dyslexia in this study, higher drawing ability does appear related to the personality measure of conscientiousness, and also both to sex (in the

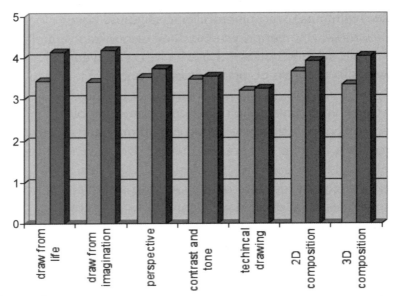

Figure 1

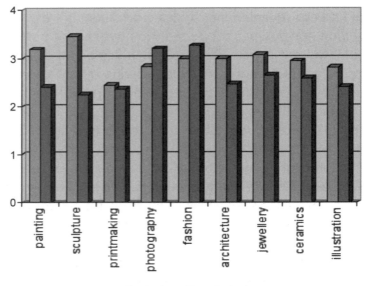

□ Dyslexic ■ Non-dyslexic

Figure 2

biological sense, males drawing better than females) and to gender (with those who perceive themselves as being more masculine drawing better, whether they are male or female). There were also indications of a correlation between a weakness in accurate objective drawing and mathematical ability, and we plan to explore these indications further in the near future. It was also found that poor drawers are less good at accurately copying angles and proportions, and their visual memory is less good.

As well as wishing to understand why some art students cannot draw well, we would also like to be able to help art students who cannot draw but wish to draw well. The above findings inform a proposed group teaching strategy for drawing, elaborated below, which attempts to empower the weaker students without hindering the progress of those who are more able.

Our research raises several possibilities. Firstly, it would appear that motivational and personality factors are important in being able to draw well, and one possibility is that increasing both motivation and the opportunity to practise

Figure 3

drawing will improve performance (as with any complex skill). Another possibility is that art students may benefit from the explicit teaching of techniques for carrying out very low level copying skills, such as in accurately representing angles and proportions: accurately perceiving angles and proportions would in itself be beneficial to all students.

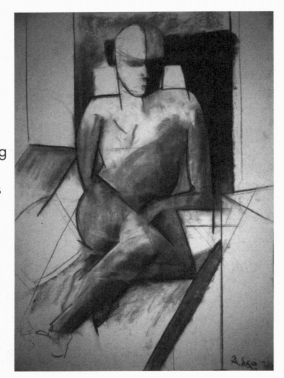

Figure 4

A strategy to implement both approaches is being considered at present. This is structured upon an eight-step teaching programme (Nist & Mealey 1991) designed to consolidate learning through the following repetitive procedures:

1 focus attention
2 give a general overview
3 introduce new terms
4 go through the procedure step by step
5 model the process – think aloud – introduce new frameworks of thought; the students also discuss the process and teach each other
6 guide the practice – students repeat the instructor's strategy

with support
7 independent practice
8 re-demonstrate the
   practice, if necessary,
   to reinforce

The eight-step process
outlined above can be
adapted to the teaching of
drawing in a traditional
life-room, where the
student is encouraged:

1 to focus attention upon
   the model and their
   relationship with the
   surroundings
   (figure/field relations –
   see figure 3)
2 to construct a general
   structure, or scaffolding,

Figure 5

in terms of drawing the main axes of the pose, using, for
example, the 'invisible grid' of lines running across the
figure that connect salient points such as nose, nipples,
navel, knees, and knuckles. These axes might be the vehicle
by which students hone their skills of accuracy in drawing
angles and lengths in proportion so that the repetitive, low-
level exercise is perceived to have contextual meaning for
the student (see figure 4)
3 to introduce visual concepts such as 'contrast boundary' in
   place of the common term 'outline'. This immediately
   engages the student with the variety of tonal values across
   the whole subject-matter and, in particular, allows the
   student to notice how the contrast boundary fluctuates at the

edges between figure and field. The concept of 'negative space' (spaces between those items in the visual field normally labelled with language), can also aid students to look without language, to apply specifically non-verbal methods in the process of drawing (see figure 5)

4 to repeat these first three steps at the beginning of every new pose

5 to discuss with the tutor the process under way on the drawing board

6 to repeat the instructor's strategy with support from the tutor

7 to draw independently at unsupervised open-access life sessions

8 to re-demonstrate the practices and strategies offered by the tutor in order to reinforce them

Could this be a helpful, inclusive model when thinking about teaching drawing processes to both dyslexic and non-dyslexic students? Plans are in hand for the probing of this question in the Foundation Diploma course at SMU, and we look forward to reporting progress.

Reference

Nist, S.L. & Mealey, D. (1991). Teacher-directed comprehension strategies. In R.F. Flippo & D.C. Caverly (Eds.) *Teaching Reading and Study Strategies at the College Level*. Newark: International Reading Association.

Qona Rankin is Dyslexia Co-ordinator at the Royal College of Art in London

Dr Howard Riley is Head of Research in Art & Design at Swansea Metropolitan University

Dyslexia and visuospatial ability: is there a causal link?

Nicola Brunswick and G. Neil Martin

One of the talents that appears to characterise developmental dyslexia is superior visuospatial ability. Several great artists, designers, architects and fashion designers, including Richard Rogers, Norman Foster, Tommy Hilfiger and Paul Smith have credited their dyslexia with helping them to realise their potential. The award-winning, furniture and product designer Sebastian Bergne, for example, noted that:

> "When you have choices, you go for what you're good at. If one part of your development is 'blocked', you develop other parts more fully. As a child I got used to expressing things in a different way to writing. I think visually. I think in pictures. If I'm designing an object, I know the exact shape in 3D. I can walk around it in my head before drawing it."

While photographer David Bailey observed:

> "I feel dyslexia gave me a privilege. It pushed me into being totally visual"

The interesting question that arises from these persuasive and impressive anecdotal examples is this: is there empirical evidence to demonstrate that dyslexia is positively and significantly associated with better visuospatial performance?

Dyslexia amongst art students, and in art and design professions

Visuospatial ability can be defined as the ability to manipulate objects mentally in three-dimensional space, and one profession or area of life in which such an ability might be essential is art and design. One study of the incidence of dyslexic students at various prestigious art colleges in England found that the figure was 10% at the Surrey Institute of Art and Design, 15% at Central St Martins College of Art and Design in London (this figure rose to over 30% for foundation students with 'dyslexia-type learning difficulties'), and 25% at London's Royal College of Art (Steffert, 1998). Similar figures have been reported for courses on fine art and design at Göteborg University in Sweden (Wolff & Lundberg, 2002).

While non-dyslexic readers with spatial talents might be as likely to choose an area of study or an occupation that demands verbal or spatial abilities, dyslexic readers with spatial talents would not have the luxury of this choice. However, it should be noted that students only gain entry to these art schools on genuine artistic merit, not because other, language-based, paths are blocked to them. Beverly Steffert, the author of one of these studies, has noted that "while most art and design students display strong visuospatial abilities, the most innovative students were often those with dyslexia".

If dyslexic readers genuinely possess superior, holistic visuospatial ability, then those who enter, and excel in, visuospatial and creative professions, might demonstrate this ability in their work. Anecdotal examples of this exist in the form of award-winning lighting and furniture designer, Terence Woodgate who observes that:

"Visualisation is one of my strengths as a designer. I think I'm particularly good with mechanisms. I can see the whole thing finished and working. I don't need paper. I like to design while driving or showering. I'm sure this is because part of my brain is distracted, leaving the creative side to dream. It's as though we dyslexics have a 3D graphics card integrated into our heads"

and John Chambers, President and CEO of Cisco Systems (the company that develops routers and software – the 'plumbing' – for the internet), who told Fortune Magazine in 2002:

"I can't explain why, but I just approach problems differently... I picture a chess game on a multiple-layer dimensional cycle and almost play it out in my mind... I don't make moves one at a time. I can usually anticipate the potential outcome and where the Ys in the road will occur. I'm very good at seeing something and memorizing the whole concept."

In the same article, biologist and inventor Bill Dreyer (whose invention of a protein-sequencing machine enabled the launch of the human genome project) expressed a similar idea as he explained the way his mind works:

"I was able to see the machine in my head and rotate valves and actually see the instrumentation... I think in 3-D Technicolor pictures instead of words. I don't think of dyslexia as a deficiency. It's like having CAD (computer-aided design) in your brain."

Recognising the impossible

In a series of experiments exploring visuospatial talent in dyslexic adults, Ellen Winner and her research group in Boston found that dyslexic readers out-performed non-dyslexic readers when they were asked to indicate whether objects drawn in two-dimensions could exist in three-dimensions (von Károlyi, Winner, Gray & Sherman, 2003; Winner, von Károlyi, Malinsky, French, Seliger, Ross, & Weber, 2001). All of the objects looked plausible on close inspection of their individual parts. Viewing each figure as a whole object, however, showed that some could not exist in the real-world – i.e. they were *impossible* figures.

Dyslexic readers were faster and no less accurate than non-dyslexic readers at recognising the impossibility of these figures. To do this, they needed to take a *global* (holistic) rather than a *local* (analytical) perspective of the images. This ability to take an overview of objects, to see things as wholes, is the skill that the authors identified as being necessary for professions such as art, engineering and architecture, in which some dyslexic readers excel.

Navigating the virtual world

Support for this idea is provided by our research (Brunswick, Martin & Marzano, 2008) in which we asked groups of dyslexic adults (10 men, 10 women, mean age = 27.6 years) and non-dyslexic adults (10 men, 11 women, mean age = 26.2 years) to complete various visuospatial and cognitive tasks. These required participants to:

■ identify objects in an ambiguous figure – e.g. a drawing that if looked at one way can be seen as a duck, while if looked at another way can be seen as a rabbit

Figure 1

- reproduce printed designs using coloured plastic blocks (the Block Design subtest of the Wechsler Adult Intelligence Scale)
- recall the direction of the queen's head on a British postage stamp (in case you're not sure, she faces left, towards the address)
- familiarise themselves with a simple, computer-based virtual reality town containing two trees and eight spatially and physically distinct buildings (a school, a block of flats, a windmill, a spiral tower building, a blue tower block, an apartment block, a garden shed, and a greenhouse – see figure 1), and then recreate the town using scale cardboard models of the buildings and a plan with the roads drawn on (see figure 2). Credit was given for showing the correct locations of the buildings relative to the town's roads and to each other.

Figure 2

We found that dyslexic men were significantly better than dyslexic women and unimpaired readers at identifying items in the ambiguous figures (see figure 3), at reproducing designs using the coloured blocks (see figure 4), and at recalling the direction of the queen's head on a stamp (see figure 5). Dyslexic men were also faster and more accurate than dyslexic women and unimpaired men at recreating the virtual reality town (see figures 6a and 6b).

These results strongly suggest that visuospatial superiority in dyslexia may be more common in men. Although male visuospatial advantage is well-reported in the research literature, only one group has previously reported similar effects of sex in dyslexic readers: Winner et al (2001) found that dyslexic men were better than dyslexic women at mentally rotating an object, and at recalling a complex printed figure.

What might these findings mean?

There are two possible explanations:
1. It could reflect a 'pathology of superiority'

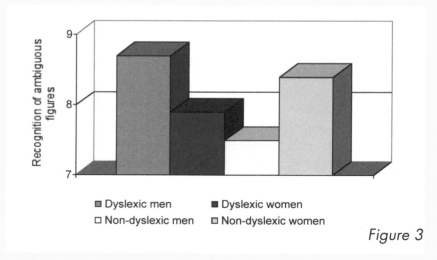

Figure 3

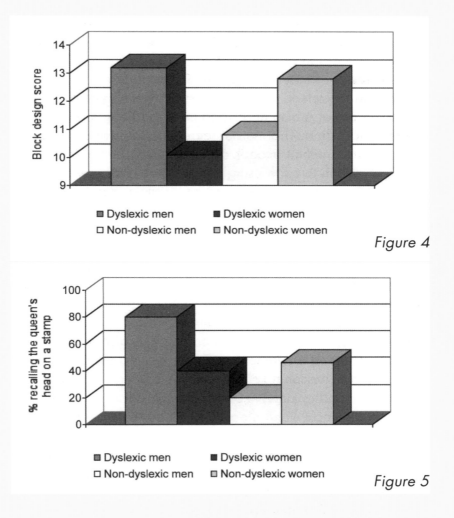

Figure 4

Figure 5

The neurologist Norman Geschwind suggested that dyslexia is associated with a 'pathology of superiority', where the right side of the brain (which is associated with holistic, spatial (non-verbal) processing) is more developed than normal because of poor development of the analytic, verbal, left side of the brain. This has been seen, post mortem, in four adult, male dyslexic readers. Of these four, in life one had been a skilled metal sculptor, one a qualified engineer, and one was 'athletically gifted'.

2. It could reflect a dyslexic processing strategy
Dyslexic readers (particularly men) may preferentially adopt a visuospatial processing style rather than a verbal processing style. That is, they may tend to solve problems by creating mental images of the problems rather than by thinking them through using words. Such a difference has been found when dyslexic and non-dyslexic readers solve syllogisms – a form of deductive reasoning consisting of:

a. a major premise, such as 'All swans are white'
b. a minor premise, 'This bird is white', and
c. a conclusion, 'This bird is a swan'.

Assuming that the major and minor premises are true, the task is to decide whether the conclusion is also true. Dyslexic men and women are more likely to adopt a visuospatial reasoning strategy when solving syllogisms (Bacon, Handley and McDonald, 2007). For example, they will draw simple Venn diagrams, with overlapping circles representing each premise. Non-dyslexic readers are more likely to adopt a verbal strategy by thinking through the possible relationships between the groups described in each premise. If men in general are disposed to develop better visuospatial skill, therefore, the greater attention paid to visuospatial functioning by dyslexic men in particular, to compensate for their verbal deficits, may partly explain our research findings.

Either of these explanations might help to explain the findings of our study, and the disproportionate numbers of dyslexic readers in art colleges and in professions such as art,

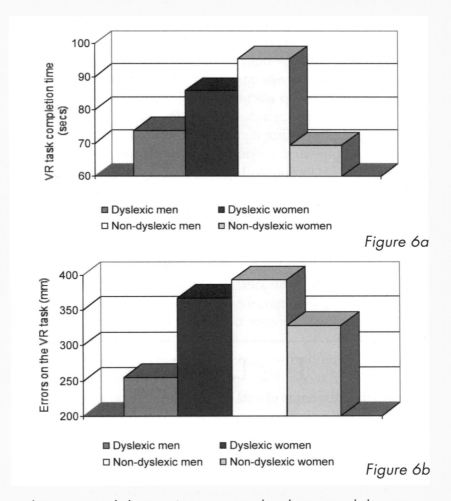

Figure 6a

Figure 6b

architecture and design. It remains to be determined, however, whether these larger than expected numbers of dyslexic artists and architects include disproportionate numbers of men.

Future studies might systematically examine the relationship between dyslexia and visuospatial ability in larger samples of dyslexic and unimpaired, male and female readers. They might include a range of tests of global and local processing to explore the possibility that dyslexic readers' visuospatial advantage may be explained by their greater ability to process information globally rather than locally (that is, whether they pay greater attention to the global object or image, rather than the elements within it).

References

Bacon, A. M., Handley, S. J., & McDonald, E. L. (2007). Reasoning and dyslexia: A spatial strategy may impede reasoning with visually rich information. *British Journal of Psychology, 98*, 79-92.

Brunswick, N., Martin, G.N. & Marzano, L. (2008). Visuospatial ability and dyslexia. Is there a male global advantage? Poster presented at the British Dyslexia Association's 7th international conference, Harrogate, 29th March.

The Dominie

55 Warriner Gardens, London SW11 4DX

- A co-educational day school for dyslexic and dyspraxic children between the ages of 6 and 13.
- Whole school approach to remedial education
- 4:1 pupil/staff ratio
- Maximum class size of 8
- CReSTeD registered Category DSP

For further information please contact:

Tel: 020 7720 8783 • Email: info@thedominie.co.uk

Steffert, B. (1998). Sign minds and design minds. In S. Dingli (Ed.), *Creative Thinking: Towards Broader Horizons.* Proceedings of the third international conference on creative thinking. Malta University Press.

von Károlyi, C., Winner, E., Gray, W., & Sherman, G.F. (2003). Dyslexia linked to talent: Global visual-spatial ability. *Brain and Language, 85*, 427-431.

Winner, E., von Károlyi, C., Malinsky, D., French, L., Seliger, C., Ross, E., & Weber, C. (2001). Dyslexia and visual-spatial talents: Compensation vs deficit model. *Brain and Language, 76*, 1, 81-110.

Wolff, U. & Lundberg, I. (2002). The prevalence of dyslexia among art students. *Dyslexia, 8*, 32-42.

Dr Nicola Brunswick and **Dr G. Neil Martin** are psychologists at the Department of Psychology, School of Health and Social Sciences, Middlesex University, Hendon, London.

Some ideas for integrating dyslexic students into dance education

Peter Lia

Introduction

Dyslexia is normally associated with reading and writing, so there is little appreciation of the difficulties that some dyslexic students face when following a course of study in dance. In fact, it is often assumed that dyslexic students excel in creative fields such as music, dance or art. In reality, dyslexic students can face the same challenges to learning as in other subject areas, as well as the same discrimination and misunderstanding from schools and teachers. Many students therefore have to develop their own coping or learning strategies. This chapter presents ideas and suggestions for teaching dance to dyslexic students.

Examples of 'reasonable adjustment' in dance education

Allowances can be made for dyslexic students to give them the same opportunity as their non-dyslexic peers. The term often used is 'reasonable adjustment', and such measures can be highly effective because even a small change can have substantial benefits when integrating dyslexic students into the dance class. Students should be encouraged to compile their own list of reasonable adjustments, but other adjustments can be more general (e.g. sympathetic consideration of spelling errors in written work) or course-specific. For example, dyslexic dance students should be:

- allowed to record sessions (audio and video are both possible)
- given lesson plans or handouts in advance so they can prepare
- allowed to wear something to help distinguish left and right
- given a suitable place in the studio, perhaps closer to the teacher
- allowed extra time for assessments

The work environment: the dance studio

The importance of the teaching environment is often highlighted in education theory but it is just as often ignored in practice. Consequently, teaching rooms tend to reflect the needs of teachers rather than their students. The work environment in dance education (the dance studio) is distinctive and flexible, and can be adapted to help students with dyslexia.

Orientation, spatial awareness or 'travelling' in a dance studio can be a problem for some dyslexic students. Often, they will use features of a room to orientate themselves (e.g. the instruction 'move to the white wall' is easier to understand than is 'move to the left'). Other possible adaptations include:

- giving each wall of the studio a distinguishing feature or colour (e.g. an object, symbol or clearly coloured shape)
- making each corner of the studio look different (this will help students to move in diagonals)
- un-cluttering studios so that distractions are limited and attention is on the teacher (this can help students with ADD in particular)

- covering full-length mirrors that are not being used in teaching as these can be a distraction
- providing good lighting, preferably natural light rather than strong artificial light

Furthermore, most students benefit from familiarity, so where possible the teacher should:

- encourage students to explore the studio before the course starts
- allow students to use the same studio throughout the course for rehearsal and assessment
- keep the 'audience' or 'stage front' side of the studio consistent
- make one part of the studio the 'off-stage area', especially immediately before a performance at a different location

The importance of the dance teacher

One study of dance students concluded with the following statement:

> *"When we asked the students about dance, all spoke at some point about dance teachers. Some of their relationships with teachers had been close, nurturing, supportive; others were characterized mainly by distance, pressure, inequality, power plays and fear. Regardless, the authority of teachers was rarely questioned." (Stinson, Blumenfield-Jones & van Dyke, 1990)*

Dance teachers often underestimate the authority and influence that they have, but it is the teacher who has the greatest potential in helping dyslexic students to integrate and learn.

The Dyslexia Teaching Centre

The Dyslexia Teaching Centre is a busy centre offering teaching and assessments in the middle of London. It provides highly qualified and specialist support for children, students and adults of all ages, enabling individuals to acquire the skills needed for success in education, the workplace and everyday life.

The multi-disciplinary team

- Specialist teachers
- Specialist assessors
- Music and art specialists
- Physiotherapists
- Educational psychologists
- Maths specialists
- Speech & language therapists
- Occupational therapists

We offer

- Educational advice
- Literacy, maths and study skills
- Touch typing classes
- Assessment at all ages
- Speech therapy
- Inset days for schools
- Support in GCSE, A level, university and professional examinations
- One-to-one tuition
- Pair and small group work
- Computer skills training
- Workplace assessments
- Motor therapy skills
- Handwriting courses

The Dyslexia Teaching Centre
23 Kensington Square, London W8 5HN

tel: 020 7361 4790 email: info@dyslexiateachingcentre.co.uk

www.dyslexiateachingcentre.co.uk

Because most dyslexic students develop their own inventive, often idiosyncratic coping strategies, they look to the teacher for acceptance, understanding and further help. A dance teacher who is aware of dyslexia, keen to help, and enthusiastic about overcoming barriers to learning, is by far the best asset that a dyslexic dance student can have.

The use of multi-sensory teaching methods

Multi-sensory education is the key to working effectively with dyslexic students, and in the context of dance education it can be practised with conviction. In fact, teaching dance offers the ideal opportunity for multi-sensory teaching and learning including observation, movement, voice, speech, music, modelling, painting, drawing, and writing. Many dance teachers practise multi-sensory techniques intuitively, but some are locked into a method of instruction that does not work for all students in a class. It is the willingness of teachers to try new approaches that achieves results. One dance teacher brought a helium-filled balloon to the dance studio and asked his students to hold it so that they could 'feel' the lift he wanted them to achieve in their jumps. A teacher's imagination is the key that unlocks the potential of multi-sensory education.

The importance of clarity in verbal expression

Dyslexic individuals can misinterpret verbal instructions, and it is inevitable that some dyslexic dance students will misunderstand certain directions no matter how clearly the teacher believes they have been given. This is illustrated in the following quotes from two dyslexic dance students:

"When they say 'go left along the diagonal', I just follow the student in front of me and hope that they know where

they are going – so I'm never at the front." – Nicola

"If someone tells me to put my leg under my knee, I can think of lots of ways to do that and I never know which one they want, so I need to see it as well as hear it." – Laura

Therefore, an awareness of dyslexia, and patience, will help teachers avoid remarks like: "what *exactly* is it you don't understand!?" When teachers become more aware of the way they speak to a class, their teaching style can improve to help the dyslexic student. To this end, it is suggested that:

■ spoken instructions are explicit and precise, preferably accompanied by actions
■ spoken instructions are also accompanied by touch to direct the student
■ details are pointed out (e.g., to focus attention on a particular part of the body, muscle or joint)
■ teachers should be prepared to repeat instructions, change the words used, and show by example

Of course, verbal instructions can also be highly visual. Some teachers use visual language naturally; for others, it may be a tool that they can develop. For example, compare:

"Keep your back straight!" "Keep a straight posture!"
with:
"Imagine that your head is being pulled upwards by a taut string that is attached to a tree branch directly above you!"
And compare:
"Keep your heels and toes on the floor!"
with:
"Your heels are glued to the floor with superglue and there is a heavy weight in your big toe that's holding it down!"

The use of visualisation

As well as the obvious visual nature of a teacher demonstrating dance moves to the students, there are many other ways to incorporate visualisation into dance teaching, for example:

- lesson plans or course outlines which include diagrams and photographs
- the effective use of colour in the studio and for handouts[1]
- video recordings of lessons which reinforce reflection and learning
- a white/black board in the studio allows the teacher to use drawings to support instruction
- students should be encouraged to draw simple stick figures with joints to help in learning moves (e.g. see figure 1); drawing can be a way of expressing ideas and is often easier than writing long, reflective logbooks (which should be avoided if possible)

Teaching dance moves

Many dyslexic students cannot easily break down sequences of moves and commit them to memory, so the initial learning phase can take longer for these students. However, with

Figure 1

From Wilmer and Lara (1998)

1 Some dyslexic individuals experience Meares-Irlen Syndrome in which the visual perception of text becomes distorted. The links between the condition and dyslexia are unproven, but many dyslexic students find that the use of coloured paper, overlays or lenses can help with reading and writing.

support and encouragement, complex arrangements can be mastered, as illustrated in the following quote from a dyslexic student:

"Once I've got the dance, I've got it really well, but if you don't give me a chance, I won't learn it." – Laura

Because all learners are individuals, there cannot be an ideal way of teaching a dance move or sequence, but a teacher's willingness to try different approaches can be key to helping dyslexic students overcome blocks to learning. Dance moves might best be taught by:

- breaking them down into sections and demonstrating each one individually (diagrams and numbers can help)
- 'chunking' the dance into numbered or named sections, with start and end points clearly identified
- demonstrating with verbal reinforcement (talking while moving if possible)
- involving more 1:1 help with touch to guide the student
- thinking of the pace (can it be done slower?)
- repeating often, especially difficult sections
- not assuming understanding (this should be checked for)
- picking out details and isolating what is going wrong, using models and diagrams to make this clear
- teaching the same move on the two legs as essentially separate moves

Some dyslexic students find it difficult to watch the teacher from the audience's perspective even when the teacher is 'mirroring' what they need to do. It may help some dyslexic students if they are allowed to watch and follow the teacher from behind or from the side. Clearly, it is not practical for dance teachers to stand with their backs to students, but on specific occasions and for a particular move, allowing a student to get a new perspective can be useful.

Contextualising the dance lesson

Many dyslexic students find practical work more rewarding than theory. Anything that grounds learning in reality or ties it to meaning or purpose is likely to help. Dance education provides numerous opportunities to contextualise learning, e.g.:

- an overview of the course outline will allow the student to see each lesson or activity as part of a larger whole
- relate the learning of dance to real works with reference to choreographers and specific pieces or performances
- invite dancers and choreographers to talk to students encourage students to choreograph (even very short pieces) as this makes direct use of learnt dance techniques
- props and costumes from a performance can give abstract dance a 'real' feeling
- talk about the students' place in the world of professional dance – how the lessons may apply to a career in dance as a performer or teacher
- before attending live performances, or when watching demonstrations by teachers or peers, prepare students with clear guidelines to focus on details that are relevant to what is being taught

The importance of review

To help dyslexic students learn dance moves, it is important that they understand not only what is being done, but why it is done in a particular way. Only with this understanding can review reinforce learning. Review can be encouraged:

- through the use of lesson plans and outlines
- through paired work as one student can remind the other
- by breaking moves down into short units
- by allowing students to record lessons
- by making work and practice schedules
- by picking students to perform to peers during class
- by including moves from previous weeks in the warm-up

The importance of music

Finding the rhythm, or identifying the beat pattern of a movement, can be difficult for many dyslexic dance students, but once it is established it can be an invaluable aid to movement memory. This is illustrated in the following quotes:

> *"It is impossible to get out of step with a tune when the stress falls with unfailing regularity on the strong beat." (Lunn, 1885)*

> *"Music has the power to embed sequences and to do this when other forms of organization (including verbal forms) fail." (Sacks, 2008, p258)*

Finding the beat can be encouraged through the use of:

- live rather than recorded music
- simple hand drums (like West African djun djuns or bongos) rather than the piano, as they focus on the beat
- music that is accessible to students so they can practise with it outside the lesson
- music recorded in digital format so it can be put onto an mp3 player

Learning dance terminology

Learning new and unusual words can be difficult for dyslexic students, as illustrated in the following quotes:

> *"I translate all those funny French words into my own language!" – Zoe*

> *"I never like those French words – they mean nothing to me" – Laura*

In learning dance terms, dyslexic students can make use of the same strategies (often visual) that they employ in improving their spelling and vocabulary. As Nicola reported, for example:

> *"I know most of the dance terms. I learnt them when I was young using pictures"*

Again, teachers can help by:

- providing students with the terminology before the class
- giving pictures, images or diagrams with the key words
- putting words in context (including them in sentences) to explain their meaning
- not giving out alphabetical lists of words but grouping words that have something in common (e.g., used to describe a particular sequence)
  not asking dyslexic students to say foreign words aloud in class
- articulating any difficult words for the student, if possible providing a recording that they can listen to later
- introducing only a small number of new words or terms in any single class

- reinforcing words that have to be learnt with movement
- looking for associations between words and the senses (e.g. *ciseaux* – the French word for scissors, sounds like scissors, and is a jump in which the legs are open to look like a pair of scissors)

Conclusion

Although most of the suggestions in this chapter have come from dyslexic dance students working at undergraduate level, many of the ideas are valid as good educational practice for all students.

Of course, some dyslexic students are 'natural' dancers and need no particular help, others may need to overcome difficulties such as poor short-term memory, lack of focus, problems with sequencing, or the inability to recognise patterns quickly. If teachers are prepared to think again when working with individual students then many of the ideas presented here can be effectively put into practice. For dyslexic students, even a small change can make a big difference.

Thanks to all the dance students who contributed ideas especially: Nicola, Zoe, Samantha and Laura

References

Lunn, H.C. (1885). The educational value of dance music. *The Musical Times and Singing Class Circular, 26, 507, 253 - 255.* Available at: http://www.jstor.org/stable/3356249

Sacks, O. (2008). *Musicophilia: Tales of Music and the Brain.* Picador: London.

Stinson, S. W., Blumenfield-Jones, D. & van Dyke, J. (1990). Voices of young women dance students: An interpretive

study of meaning. *Dance Research Journal, 22*, 2, 13-22.
Available at: http://www.jstor.org/stable/1477780
Wilmer, C. & Lara, C. (1998). Illustrations and nomenclature
stave for dance movements: What visual communication
can do for dance. *Leonardo, 31*, 2, 111-117. Available at:
http://www.jstor.org/stable/1576513

Peter Lia is a Learning Support Tutor at Middlesex University
in North London

The impact of dyslexia on the dance student: bringing the practical into practice

Nanette Kincaid

During my years working as a professional dancer, teacher and choreographer, I had never encountered dyslexia being offered as a reason for difficulties in processing and retaining material. Up until that point, I presumed that dyslexia was exclusively related to reading and writing difficulties and had no impact on practically-based work.

After working for five years within Higher Education, I decided to embark on a practice-as-research study to investigate if there were other considerations that I needed to understand as I felt that I had possibly misunderstood a percentage of my students.

The practical implications of dealing with a learning difficulty within dance are not widely considered or even recognised. Most professional dance teachers are unaware that dyslexia can have an impact on one's balance, proprioception (unconscious awareness of the location of one's body in space), co-ordination, sequencing, mirroring skills and short-term memory.

Having said that, even the dyslexic dance student can be unaware of these related difficulties, and most put it down to them 'just not being very good'. This comment reveals what I believe to be one of the most influential factors in this condition: low self-confidence which unintentionally leads to self-imposed learning blocks. This is highlighted by Dennison and Dennison (1989) in the following way:

"We believe that there are no learning disabilities, only learning blocks. We are all learning blocked to some extent that we have mastered the art of not moving."

I believe there is a need to bring in practical tools and defined strategies or guidelines to a dance class. A traditionally taught technique class cannot stay regimented. There is still huge value in this way of teaching and learning, indeed it is essential, as in the 'real world' this is the way in which students will usually gain employment at auditions. I believe that practically taught subjects should also embrace new ideas in order to keep evolving.

Context

The main theories I have worked with include those of Paul Dennison, founder of Brain Gym and Educational Kinesiology (www.braingym.org.uk/). He states the importance of using cross lateral movement to develop more effective neural pathways in bridging the hemisphericDivide. Dennison's work also connects with that of Peter Blythe and Sally Goddard Blythe of the Institute of Neuro-Physiological Psychology (www.inpp.org.uk/) who state that 'Movement is the key to learning'.

Heavily tied to the above work is Nicolson and Fawcett's (1990) cerebellar deficit theory of dyslexia which suggests that there is a mild dysfunction to the cerebellum; this is a structure at the back of the brain which is involved in the co-ordination of movements as well as in some aspects of language processing. Research into the role of the cerebellum has helped to explain why some people with dyslexia appear to have a surprising number of difficulties in areas other than literacy – such as balance, motor co-ordination, speed of processing and other functions which are controlled by the cerebellum.

Viable aids and strategies

The Floor Compass™

This is a visual teaching and learning aid which I have developed after recognising the problems that some of my students were having with understanding basic directional instructions. The time needed for the dyslexic student to understand which direction to move towards meant that they were already a few steps behind the group, and always trying to catch up. It is little wonder that these students chose to 'hide' at the back of the class, thus further reducing their already low confidence levels.

In its simplest explanation, the Floor Compass™ is different coloured lines on a square of floor within a golden circle. By using colour references, I am attempting to aid the sensory input which helps form memory, reinforcing its effectiveness in offering multi-sensory triggers for the memory. The Floor Compass™ also seems to aid 'serial memory' as suggested by Cratty (1969) who noted that using visual cues, even if placed in a different environment, enhanced recollection of a task.

One of my main observations is that the Floor Compass™ delivers the most effective results when combined with appropriate aural information, again attempting to create as many sensory triggers as possible (Orton-Gilligham, 1930). The language appears to enable the student to internalize their understanding, and connect the dots, rather than always just imitating. For example, rather than giving the instruction 'tilt to the right, into a diagonal curve', I would now say something like, 'tilt the shoulders to the white line on the red side, slowly roll off and finish hanging the arms either side of the front red diagonal line, noticing that your nose is now directly over the red line'.

My theory on the Floor Compass™ is that it helps to develop a greater sense of 'self' in space, and contributes to the development of spatial and directional awareness by providing a tangible, visual learning aid. This has shown a deepened understanding by the student (similar to Laban's theories on Space, Checchetti's Points in Space, and Eshkol-Wachman's Movement Notation). This also allows for preferred methods of learning (visual, aural and kinesthetic), and helps the student to develop a mental image of the space as a whole that they can work with later on in the class, when 'travelling' (moving around the available space) for example.

The Visual Scribe

This device – which is, in its most basic form, a podcast – offers the student a chance to watch filmed recordings of their own class performance, allowing them more time to reflect and process comments from the tutor. It offers a valuable resource which helps the student to assimilate the teacher's corrections and feedback with their own self-perceptions.

It also encourages the student to recognise the moment(s) where they may lose concentration and/or understanding of the material. This is an important step to make as focusing on completing the movement even just one count further will contribute towards developing greater physical and mental stamina.

The dyslexic dancer can be in danger of unintentionally introducing blocks to movement phrases, for example, every time that they struggle to remember what comes next in the sequence, they are actually deepening that particular hesitation into their movement. It is essential to have a 'smooth' recollection from memory to body in order to have fluid movement quality. So, to focus on increasing the retention of material even a few counts further every time will help to develop this smoother transition.

The instructional DVD

It appeared very unbalanced that dance students did not have reference guides specifically for the technique classes in which they participated. I believe that in order to make the University experience a more fully formed and cohesive process for the dyslexic dance student, a symbiotic relationship between practice and theory needs to be better established.

As part of my research I filmed a prototype DVD which offers front and back view demonstrations of the class exercises to music, as well as front and back view verbal demonstrations (to allow for preferred methods of learning). For example, the warm-up can be viewed with the 'front view with music' choice. This allows the student to work in their own time on a particular section that they may be struggling to process and/or retain. This DVD is being further developed to include chapters on how to approach basic elements from my class, and for guidelines on using the Floor Compass™ as well as a newly devised pre-class warm-up using the Floor Compass™, a balance board and bean bags.

Initiating exercises on the left side

As a teacher I habitually taught exercises starting on the right side without even questioning why. Researching this area it occurred to me that it may actually be more beneficial to start exercises on the left side to tap into the creative 'whole idea' concept as well as rhythm and movement; these are thought to be processed in the right hemisphere of the brain (the right hemisphere also controls movement of the left side of the body). I have observed that even the thought process involved in the student breaking from the habitual muscle memory and starting on the 'other side' produces a significant increase in their concentration and ability.

Increased use of cross-lateral movement

I have also started to introduce more 'basic' movements (crawling, walking and balancing) in the warm-up stage of class. By attempting to re-train the neural pathways and build more efficient synaptic connections, the mind-body connection is encouraged to strengthen and develop which provides the possibility to understand more complex material further into the class. By using a basic crawling pattern the brain is required to bridge 'the hemisphericDivide', transferring information from one side of the brain to the opposite side of the body very rapidly.

Encouraging bi-lateral transfer of motor skills

Teaching and learning new material is a time consuming business which is why it makes sense to start on the usually weaker left side. Having said that, it is generally accepted in technique classes that the student transfers the material to the other side by themselves often in a much shorter period of time.

This can seem like a monumental task for the dyslexic student as it can feel like trying to learn the phrase from scratch again, with hardly any recollection of what has just been learnt on the other side of the body. Those students who are able to transfer the material independently free up the teacher who can then begin the process on the other side with the students who require further support.

It is worth noting that the students should still be encouraged to work at the transference, processing and retention of material by themselves as much as possible, to avoid the teacher becoming a 'Zimmer frame' and actually starting to restrict (albeit through good intentions) the student's ability to work independently.

Association, visualisation and mnemonics

The majority of dyslexic students learn with greater ease using imagery, visualization and/or mnemonics (a memory aid such as a short poem or special word). For example, when demonstrating a high arch, I use the image of a wine glass. This produces a clear visual reference, especially when working on a diagonal, and I inform the students that the wine is pouring out of their glass all over the floor as their shoulders are uneven or not 'square'.

Increasing the frequency with which I use these devices appears to have had a beneficial impact on the students' ability to retain information and maintain focus. Of even more value is that such a skill can also be easily implemented by the student themselves.

Emotional learning

When some members of my focus group referred to taking class as 'Survival', I understood a little more about the potential emotional barriers that may be related to their low self-confidence. In Dennison's theories, a structure at the base of the brain called the brain stem is responsible for forward and backward motion (based on the fundamental survival concept of 'fight or flight'). Dennison states that the 'tendon-guard reflex', which shortens the tendons from the head to the heels in preparation for flight, is activated by the brainstem when we are in unfamiliar learning situations; this confounds the vestibular system and spatial awareness.

After some reflection, I realised that the majority of dyslexic dance students were unconsciously exhibiting signs of this reflex in their posture throughout class; I would often comment that their weight was 'in their heels'. Perhaps this is a prime example of a state of mind being reflected in the body?

Some dyslexic dancers have commented that they struggle to gain sufficient 'muscle memory' (memory for specific movements) as movement is always copied as opposed to being internalised and truly understood. Dyslexic dance students whom I have interviewed describe feeling lost and disorientated when they perform without someone in front of them. Is this because of the way in which they learnt the phrase, so to lose the visual stimulus means that they then have no triggers for the memory? If so, this may explain why a lot of the dyslexic students, who choose to stay at the back of class to copy their peers, find it hard to move beyond this way of learning in dance. Perhaps one difference between dyslexic and non-dyslexic dance students is that the non-dyslexic students are better able to make the transition from mind to body, laying down the necessary routines; in other words, transferring movements from short-term to long-term memory.

Conclusion

I feel very strongly that even with all the aids and support available, a student will not be able to reach their full potential unless they take responsibility for their own learning. This applies to any student, dyslexic or not.

By taking responsibility, the student chooses to:

- avoid always staying at the back of the class (relying on others);
- arrive early to have time to 'over-learn' material (a strategy that most dyslexic readers develop from very early on);
- take their turn to perform material at the end of the group, thus allowing for slightly more processing and practice time;
- understand and recognise the way in which they learn most effectively, for example, watching the teacher from the front or back, developing personal mnemonics/imagery etc.

There are so many choices that can be implemented without really making a statement about dyslexia, and which are solely viewed as a focused, confident and mature approach to study. Until the student fully commits and does not hide behind their clothes, their hair, their label of dyslexia, they will never progress to the dizzying heights of their own capabilities, irrespective whether they have dyslexia or not.

References and further resources:

Ayres, A.J. (2005). *Sensory Integration and the Child.* Los Angeles: Western Psychological Services

Bourne, C. (2004). *Learning Difficulties in Practical Dance Study* (Final Project Report). London: Palatine

Clarkson, P. & Skrinar, M. (Eds.) (1988). *Science of Dance Training.* Illinois: Human Kinetics

Cratty, B. (1969). *Movement, Perception and Thought.* California: Peek Publications

Dennison, P. & Dennison, G. (1989). *Brain Gym Handbook.* California: Edu-Kinesthetics

Franklin, E. (1996). *Dynamic Alignment through Imagery* USA: Human Kinetics

Goddard Blythe, S. (1996). *The Role of the Cerebellum in Learning.* Presented at the 8th European Conference of Neuro-developmental Delay in Children, Chester, UK

Goddard Blythe, S. (1998). *Neurological Dysfunction in Children with Specific Learning Difficulties.* The Irish Learning Support Association Journal

Nicolson, R.I. & Fawcett, A.J. (1990). Automaticity: a new framework for dyslexia research? *Cognition, 30,* 159-182.

Taylor, J. & Taylor, C. (1995). *Psychology of Dance.* USA: Human Kinetics

Nanette Kincaid teaches in the Dance Department at the University of Chichester and is presenting her research at conferences in Britain and America. She has been fortunate enough to secure development awards from The TechDis HEAT Scheme and PALATINE to investigate this topic further.

For more information about classes or workshops, or to purchase a Floor Compass™, please contact Nanette Kincaid by email: nanettekincaid@hotmail.com

Music, Dyslexia and Language

Paula Bishop-Liebler and Katie Overy

There is growing awareness amongst researchers, teachers, parents and musicians of potential links between music and dyslexia, from both musical and language-based perspectives. Such links are perhaps not surprising when one considers some of the similarities between music and language. For example, both music and language are complex forms of communication involving small units of sound combined into long sequences, thus requiring complex auditory processing skills, sustained attention and short term memory skills. In addition, both music and language are notated visually, and require hundreds of hours of training in order to achieve fluency.

In this chapter, we examine the potential relationship between dyslexia and music from different perspectives. We begin with a short discussion of some of the difficulties with musical learning that people with dyslexia can experience. The main part of the chapter then provides practical suggestions as to how to support musicians with dyslexia, particularly in the conservatoire setting. Finally, we briefly discuss the potential use of musical activities as a way of supporting and developing language and literacy skills for children with dyslexia.

Dyslexia and musical difficulties

Many dyslexic children and adults are extremely good musicians, so there is no question of dyslexia preventing anyone from becoming a musician. However, a variety of reports have suggested that those with developmental dyslexia can experience specific difficulties with musical skills. For

example, in 1994 a study involving a number of case studies
of dyslexic musicians found that they all reported difficulties
with notation, sight-reading and rhythm (Ganschow et al,
1994). In 1995 the BDA Music Committee outlined a variety
of common problem areas including notation learning and
sight-reading, as well as confusions over Italian terminology
such as *allegro*, *allargando* and *andante*. In 1996 Sheila
Oglethorpe published a book which discussed potential
difficulties when learning to play the piano, including
problems with fine motor control, hand independence, and
maintaining a steady beat (Oglethorpe, 1996). Psychology
research has suggested that children with dyslexia can
experience difficulties with musical notation (Jaarsmal et al,
1998) and with rhythm skills (e.g. Wolff, 2002, Overy et al,
2003). Research with students at conservatoire level is
currently in its early stages, but initial findings are in line with
the reports above – music students who report difficulties with
literacy skills have been found to be more likely to report
difficulties with aspects of musical processing (Bishop-Liebler,
2004).

Of course, the way in which dyslexia is defined continues to
be debated and is an important aspect of any work in this
area, since different studies can use different definitions. Thus,
researchers are continuing to refine our understanding of the
possible relationship between dyslexia and musical learning.
Meanwhile, teachers continue to work with dyslexic students to
help them overcome their difficulties and maximise their
strengths.

Supporting musicians with dyslexia

Fortunately, within music teaching practice there is a growing
awareness of strategies that can be used to support musical

learning for individuals with dyslexia (see Sheila Oglethorpe's chapter in this handbook). In particular, multisensory techniques employed in teaching literacy and numeracy are being successfully adapted for the teaching of music (e.g. Oglethorpe, 1996, 2002; Miles et al, 2001, 2008). Less discussed are the more general issues that surround musical learning, such as institutional support systems, and organisational and time management skills. These issues are important aspects of support for any student with a specific learning difficulty and can set the scene for enabling students to access their musical learning effectively. This section describes some different ways in which students can be supported.

1. Support systems: the importance of communication

In practical terms, increasing communication between different institutional departments and individuals is a first and crucial step. This communication needs to flow in all directions. For example, music teachers are in a good position to observe the learning behaviours of students and to pick up on any difficulties that students may be experiencing, both musical and non-musical. Conversely, the Special Educational Needs Co-ordinator (SENCO) and non-musical departments may have knowledge of a student's difficulties and perhaps access to a diagnostic report, which may be extremely useful for the music teacher. Another way to encourage communication is for music teachers to include a question regarding specific learning difficulties in their initial questionnaire or discussion when starting tuition. Or, if working within a school, the music teacher can make a point of asking the appropriate person in the music department what the school's policy is with regard to confidentiality and dissemination of information regarding dyslexia/dyspraxia and disabilities. It may also be useful for diagnostic assessors such as educational psychologists and specialist teachers to consider musical learning within their assessments, for example by asking whether the student plays a musical instrument and if so, whether they experience any particular difficulties in this area.

2. Organisational and time management skills

For the individual student, difficulties with organisation and time management are often part of the dyslexic profile. For these students it is important to address such issues as early as possible, since learning cannot take place if the student is not in the lesson (!), and effective learning can be hampered if the student has not brought the correct things with them, or has not practised enough or effectively. Working with conservatoire level musicians highlights the importance of addressing these issues. If musicians are not organised they can struggle in the professional world and can experience difficulties on their course. Stress levels are often increased for musicians who are not well organised, since they are often working to strict deadlines. Also, these musicians may not be able to take up valuable opportunities such as outside engagements, since they need to be organised enough to fit unexpected events into their busy schedule.

Helping students to develop routines that are manageable and sustainable is extremely worthwhile. However, the aim is always to help the student to be independent, so any strategy requiring the input of other people needs to be short-term and targeted. For example, texting a student half an hour before their lesson may be a useful strategy at first, but it is not a long-term solution. Self awareness is perhaps the first step to good organisation and time management skills. Listed below are a few of the main areas of difficulty and some simple suggestions for support:

- *Getting to lessons on time*
  Ensure that the student knows how long it takes to get from one class to another, and then ensure that the student writes the travelling time in their schedule/diary.

- *Remembering to take the correct music and instrument to the lesson*
  Combine a lesson and practice diary together in one book, and write in the diary what the student needs to bring to the next lesson.

- *Remembering what to practise*
  During the lesson, write everything down for the student in their practice diary. This will also help with unusual spellings of composers or pieces.

- *Getting practice done*
  Help the student to schedule their practice. If the student doesn't have a schedule, creating one can help them to see how their life fits together. If the student is being supported with one-to-one dyslexia support, this may be a useful activity for those lessons.

- *Practising effectively*
  Spend a lesson or more going through practice strategies and 'observing' the student practising. Use a lesson/practice diary in which the student writes during every practice, and review it with them at the beginning of each lesson.

- *Fitting in musical activities alongside other academic work*

Having an overall schedule will help with monitoring the balance between musical and academic work. Having termly or yearly goals can also help a student to feel more motivated and in control.

■ *Filling in forms to apply for exams, competitions etc*
Put application deadlines into a student's schedule/diary, even if the parent or teacher will be completing the forms. This will help the student to understand the process, and prepare them for when they will need to complete forms themselves.

■ *Taking books/music back to the library on time*
Once again, putting due dates into a student's schedule/ diary will help to ensure that fines do not build up.

3. Use of technology

There are many ways in which technology can be used to support musical learning. Listed below are just a few ideas:

■ Use recordings at different stages of the learning process
■ Scan music into *Sibelius*, so that students can listen and read the music simultaneously – this enables them to check the accuracy of their playing
■ Record lyrics for singers to ensure that language learning is accurate from the beginning
■ For jazz musicians, use transcription software such as *Transcribe* to slow down recordings in conjunction with *Sibelius*, to check for accuracy

4. The future: an integrated approach

To support effectively the musical learning of those with

dyslexia, an integrated approach is needed which incorporates both musical and general learning (illustrated in figure 1). This means ensuring that musical learning is considered by professionals such as educational psychologists when they assess students, and that external bodies such as music examination boards consider the needs of musicians with dyslexia. When developing organisation and time management skills with a student, music lessons should be considered. Parents should be aware of the issues that dyslexic musicians may face, and should have strategies to help support their child's musical learning at home. Music teachers should be aware of the difficulties that some students may face, and of the multisensory teaching methods that can support learning. Up-to-date information regarding the use of technology for musical learning should be sought and shared. All of these areas of support can only be effectively developed with good communication between all parties.

Supporting language skills with music

The fact that children and adults with dyslexia can experience difficulties with aspects of musical learning is just one example of the many and varied potential links between music and language abilities. For example, experimental research has shown that trained musicians can have particularly good verbal memory, while neuroscientists have discovered shared neural systems for music and language processing. Language teachers and speech therapists often report using music and singing in their practice, and it has even been found that musicians have stronger neural responses to language stimuli than non-musicians (see Patel, 2008; Overy 2008a for reviews in this area).

A few educators and researchers have thus proposed that

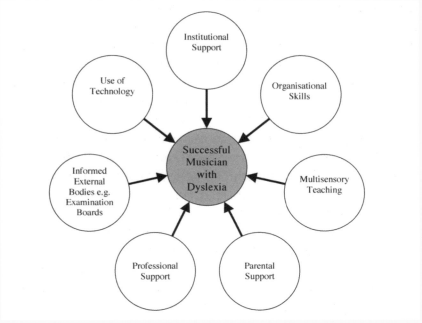

Figure 1

children with literacy difficulties might actually benefit from musical training; for example, it has been suggested that children with dyslexia might benefit from timing-based or rhythm-based musical activities in support of their auditory processing skills, phonological skills and literacy skills (Overy 2003, 2008b). This idea is gaining support amongst psychologists and neuroscientists who are exploring the potential for music to be used as an intervention tool for dyslexic children, based on a variety of evidence that musical training may lead to improved language processing skills (e.g. Tallal and Gaab, 2006). Future work in this area could prove extremely valuable for children with dyslexia – music is potentially such an enjoyable, sociable activity that it can be used extremely effectively both inside and outside the classroom, with endless opportunities for creativity and fun.

References

British Dyslexia Association Music Committee (1995). *Music and Dyslexia*. British Dyslexia Association

Bishop-Liebler, P. (2004). *Pilot Study of music and dyslexia in a conservatoire setting*. Poster presented at the BDA International Conference, York

Ganschow, L., Lloyd-Jones, J. & Miles, T.R. (1994). Dyslexia and musical notation. *Annals of Dyslexia, 44*, 185-202

Jaarsma, B. S., Ruijssenaars, A.J.J.M. & Van der Broeck, W. (1998). Dyslexia and learning musical notation: A pilot study. *Annals of Dyslexia, 48*, 137-154.

Miles, T.M., Westcombe, J. & Ditchfield, D. (Eds.) (2008). *Music & Dyslexia: A Positive Approach*. Oxford: Wiley-Blackwell

Miles, T.M. & Westcombe, J. (Eds) (2001). *Music & Dyslexia: Opening New Doors*. Oxford: Wiley-Blackwell

Oglethorpe, S. (1996, 2002). *Instrumental music for dyslexics: A teaching handbook. (1st and 2nd editions.)* London: Whurr Publishers

Overy, K. (2003). Dyslexia and Music. From Timing Deficits to Musical Intervention. In Avanzini, G., Faienza, C., Lopez, L., Majno, M., & Minciacchi, D. (Eds) The Neurosciences and Music. *Annals of the New York Academy of Sciences, 999, 497-505*

Overy, K. (2008a). Insights from brain imaging. In: Westcombe, J, Miles, T & Ditchfield, D. (Eds). *Music and Dyslexia: A Positive Approach*. Oxford: Wiley-Blackwell

Overy, K. (2008b). Classroom rhythm games for literacy support. In: Westcombe, J, Miles, T & Ditchfield, D. (Eds). *Music and Dyslexia: A Positive Approach*. Oxford: Wiley-Blackwell

Overy, K., Nicolson, R.I., Fawcett, A.J., & Clarke, E.F. (2003). Dyslexia and Music: Measuring Musical Timing Skills.

Dyslexia, 9, 18-36

Tallal, P. & Gaab, N. (2006). Dynamic auditory processing, musical experience and language development. *Trends in Neurosciences, 29, 7,* 382-390

Wolff, P.H. (2002). Timing precision and rhythm in developmental dyslexia. *Reading and Writing; an interdisciplinary journal, 15,* 179-206

Software

Sibelius is produced by Sibelius and more information can be found at www.sibelius.com

Transcribe software can be purchased from www.seventhstring.com

Paula Bishop-Liebler is a Doctoral student at the Institute of Education, London

Dr Katie Overy is a Senior Lecturer in Music at the University of Edinburgh

Music and dyslexia: Thoughts for parents and teachers

Sheila Oglethorpe

"Some of my best pupils are dyslexic" said a brass teacher when the parents of a small boy thought that it would be sensible to mention his dyslexia when selecting an instrument for him to play (Gilpin, 2001). Many instrumental music teachers use the term "musical" about their pupils even when they are having difficulty teaching them in the way they are accustomed to teach. They tend to say something along the lines of:

> "He seems quite (or very) musical but he cannot (or will not) take the trouble to read the music."

Parents also are heard to say:

> "He spends hours sitting at the piano (or fiddling about on his guitar etc.) so I am sure he is musical but he never seems to practise properly."

Both teachers and parents are often mystified when it is clear that the child is both musical and not unintelligent but (s)he seems extremely slow to grasp the connection between the sounds (s)he is making and the notes written on the page.

The clue to what is usually going on here is in the words *read the music.* It is true that there are large numbers of pupils who, while being extremely sensitive to the *sounds* of music, nevertheless find that deciphering musical notation and understanding the musical lexicon is particularly hard. A pilot study of a small group of dyslexic and non-dyslexic musicians at conservatoire level found that those who had difficulty with literacy skills also reported difficulties with aspects of musical processing such as harmony and sight reading. They did not report the same level of difficulty with written aural tests (Bishop-Liebler, 2004). The late Professor Tim Miles stressed the importance of the distinction between the sounds of music and musical notation when he wrote about musical ability in his book, *Music and Dyslexia: Opening New Doors* (2001).

Talent

It has been noted that musical talent is the gift which emerges earlier than any other (Gardner, 1983). Even babies in the womb have reacted positively to music. Talent seems to be in the genes (though there are instances of musicians who deny that they have any musical forbears, for example the world famous 20th century pianist Arthur Rubinstein who said that nobody in his family had the slightest musical gift). Dyslexia is also known to run in families, and there are many dyslexic musicians. Sometimes it is tempting to wonder if being dyslexic is a *sine qua non* for being a good musician! However there are also plenty of wonderful musicians who would never be classified as dyslexic.

I have heard it said that many dyslexic readers who are engaged in the arts are there because they are not capable of doing anything else: their dyslexic traits are too overwhelming to enable them to compete with non-dyslexic people. I contend that of all the arts, music demands more dedication than any other: the hours of practice needed to reach technical competence on an instrument are awesome. There is something about music that will not let the talented person go. Gardner (1983) also says that it is the composer's lot constantly to be monitoring and reworking tones, rhythms and larger musical patterns.

It is interesting to note that perseverance is one of the traits that has also been observed in children and adults with dyslexia, possibly ..... probably ...... because they have learnt that success in anything will only follow excessively hard work. Dyslexic people sometimes develop the habit of perseverance, so much so that their non-dyslexic relations and friends often get quite wearied by them!

Why read music?

There are good reasons why one should learn to read music. There are pockets all over the world where music is learnt aurally and many folk, pop and jazz musicians are musically illiterate, but it has become the custom in the western world for music to be passed down to the next generation by means of printed symbols on the page. Recordings, which were introduced over a century ago, do not allow for the performer's occasional embellishment or flights of freedom. Only by being able to read what composers wrote down many centuries ago, before the advent of recorded music, can we be sure that the music is reproduced faithfully.

Comparisons with reading words

There is ample evidence that there are very many musical children with learning difficulties, or *learning differences* (which is a much nicer definition), who find that their urge to discover the joys of music takes on a completely different aspect when they find that they have to follow the well-trodden paths of traditional music education. This usually means that at some early stage, if not right from the beginning, their teacher

All your Dyslexia screening needs can be fulfilled with this battery of bestselling tests

expects that they learn to read music as one would read words. In the end most dyslexic people, given the right help, usually learn to read words adequately enough to survive in the adult world. Some eventually enjoy it very much because of the way it opens up new worlds and stimulates the imagination. Some may never enjoy reading and may avoid it whenever possible.

The musical dyslexic is the same: (s)he may never be able to read music well at sight, particularly because it entails sticking to the pulse beat (there is an inexorable and unnerving ticking of the clock going on from the outset of the exercise), but not being able to sight read a piece of music does not mean that that piece cannot become part of their repertoire. If they have been taught the basic rudiments of music, and also have access to a recording of it, with patience and persistence they will eventually be able to work it out.

When a child learns to read (s)he gradually learns the sound of all 26 letters of the alphabet, and apart from a handful of look-and-say words,(s)he learns to sound out carefully each letter before stringing them together to determine what the word is. This can be an incredibly laborious process. After a while (s)he gets better at recognising groups of letters and at making good guesses from contextual clues as to what the word might be. *You cannot do this with music.* There are few comparable contextual clues (though an already experienced sight reader will get very good at guessing) and, in addition, there is the complication of rhythm. Pupils too often worry about what each note is, as they have been taught to do when reading words. Usually this method ends up at a complete halt.

The problems

What are the main questions and concerns commonly expressed by pupils with learning differences?

- "Sounds are sounds, so why is it necessary to give them names?" It is difficult to appreciate the link between written words and sounds made on an instrument
- "If sounds have to have names, why do they have to be alphabetic?" Alphabetic names may have associations the pupils do not want to revisit
- "Finger numbers muddle me up". Dyscalculic people have an aversion to numbers because they cannot relate to, or characterise, the shape of the symbol
- "Why is this sound higher than this one? For me it is just different". The words "up" and "down" or "high" and "low" may have other connotations[1]
- "I don't think of music going across a page made up of lots of black and white lines with other lines crossing them, and lots of little black dots." For many a musically talented dyslexic pupil, as soon as a book of tunes or a primer is introduced, the score gets in the way of the music.

Primers are much more colourful and have larger print these days but they still tend to try and introduce too much information. In general, the greater the number of words the more the child who learns differently feels challenged and threatened. Repetition and correction of "mistakes" then reduces music to something heavy and dull.

Creativity

Learning to read music means learning the rules, while playing music means both creatively applying and then breaking the

1 One pupil of mine thought of high sounds as being light and low sounds being dark, as in "Turn the light down". So, going from up to down meant getting darker.

rules. Thomas West (1997) suggests that creativity may be fundamental to the dyslexic brain. In fact he mentions that for Einstein, perhaps the most famous dyslexic person the world has ever known, music was extremely important all his life.

The perception of music that so many dyslexic musicians seem to have, as I understand it, can perhaps best be described as a three dimensional web of shifting colours and sounds. They are in the middle of it all. They tend not to have linear thoughts, and listening to a piece of music is for them a more multifaceted experience than it is for the non-dyslexic reader.

A pupil who has a dyslexic perception of music will have problems that must be addressed most carefully or frustration will soon set in when they are faced with what appear to be insurmountable and incredibly boring obstacles. One 11 year old boy for example, said

> *"A fuse in my mind blows... something in there wants to leap out and start playing a Mozart symphony... "*
> *(Wiltshire, 2001).*

Unfortunately, many pieces for beginners are too babyish and dull so they stifle creativity.

Reconciling creativity and the score

Practising will inevitably be devastatingly boring if most of the time it means learning to obey the rules. Practice in matching the sound to the score can, and I believe should, begin early but in that order – sound first. Make the sound and eventually see what it looks like on the page. Allow the pupil to learn pieces from memory in the lesson, practise them at home and only show them what the sounds look like on paper later when they are ready for it. Simple tunes with lots of repetition like "Frère Jacques" or "Twinkle, twinkle little star" can be used. These can be played in different keys just to get the pupil used to the shape, not the individual notes. I remember a boy that I taught this way, although he had learnt for some time with a conventional teacher, saying:

> *"Oh I see, when it goes down it means that you must go down."*

I had assumed (never assume anything!) that he had connected the shapes on the page with what he was doing with his fingers. The only thing to do, in order to read passably at sight, is to look at the general shape first and at the details later.

Duets can be introduced almost from the very beginning. They are immensely satisfying, particularly on the piano but actually on any instrument, the teacher playing alongside the pupil. Remember chopsticks? Set up a rhythm and then play together, having chosen a small selection of sounds for the pupil to play, as one would when learning jazz. Play as if you were too tired to get out of bed, play as if you were cross, play as if you were happy, play loudly, play softly, crescendo, diminuendo, and finish with a massive accelerando! Music must live!!

The role of the parent

The role of the parent of a dyslexic pupil is vital. Particularly if the teacher is cooperative they can, among other things:

- make sure that their child arrives at the lesson on time and with all the right equipment
- sit in on lessons, as all Suzuki method parents do
- make notes of what is to be practised
- help to build their child's confidence by picking up on

anything that the teacher praised in the lesson and
reminding him/her of it
■ make sure that the score, if one is being used, is enlarged
and printed on the coloured paper of their child's choice
■ remind him/her to do things like shutting his/her eyes
■ generally help with the practice but make sure that the pupil
also has time to play about and experiment with music

Only a parent can appreciate the strength of will that their
child will need, both to come to terms with their dyslexia and
also to rise above it so that their talent is developed to its full
capacity. Sometimes music can be the greatest fount of their
self esteem and we all know that without a degree of self
esteem one can do nothing.

References

Bishop-Liebler, P. (2004). *A pilot survey of dyslexia and music
in a conservatoire setting.* Poster presented at the 6ᵗʰ BDA
International conference, University of Warwick

Gardner, H. (1983). *Frames of Mind. The Theory of Multiple
Intelligencies.* New York: Basic Books

Gilpin, S. (2001). John and his cornet. In T.R. Miles and J.
Westcombe (Eds.) *Music and Dyslexia: Opening New
Doors.* Oxford: Wiley-Blackwell

Miles, T.R. (2001). The manifestations of dyslexia, its
biological bases, and its effects on daily living. In T.R. Miles
and J. Westcombe (Eds.) *Music and Dyslexia: Opening
New Doors.* Oxford: Wiley-Blackwell

West, T.G. (1997). *In the Mind's Eye.* Amherst, NY:
Prometheus Books

Wiltshire, J. (2001). A struggle to play. In T.R. Miles and J.
Westcombe (Eds.) *Music and Dyslexia: Opening New
Doors.* Oxford: Wiley-Blackwell

Sheila Oglethorpe is music/dyslexia consultant at Salisbury Cathedral School, and Chair of the BDA's Music committee. She has been a visiting lecturer on the Associated Board's CT (Certificate of Teaching) course since 1996, and she is the author of *Instrumental Music for Dyslexics*, a Teaching Handbook (published by Whurr).

Reports from the BDA Committees

Report from the Accreditation Board

Mike Johnson

On its web site there is the claim that:

> *"The BDA promotes early identification and support in schools to ensure opportunity to learn for dyslexic learners. We want to represent the needs of dyslexic people on leaving school, in higher education and in work."*

Crucial to these aims is the work of the Accreditation Board. It was set up to regularise the content and quality of courses to be accepted by the BDA as effective in training people to recognise and ameliorate dyslexia in children and young people. This was at a time when dyslexia was still a matter of 'belief' (or, in many cases non-belief!) for many in schools, colleges and local authorities.

The approach of 'consensus amongst peers' has characterised the work of the Board ever since. As the range of institutions and organisations providing professional development in dyslexia has widened, so has the membership of the Board. It has been helped in this by the fact that its awards have no authority other than their reputation. This has meant that the consensus within the Board has to be maintained externally with its 'clients' – those who employ the services of professionals working with dyslexic people. It is, therefore, apolitical in the widest sense. Dyslexia Action, PATOSS and NVQ providers are represented on the Board of 15 members. The majority of the rest are current course providers with the addition of a small number co-opted for their wider knowledge of dyslexia.

The main body of its work is overseeing courses preparing participants to apply for one of the awards of the BDA. The 'Gold Standard' is AMBDA – Associate Member of the BDA. This requires successful completion of a course delivering 90 hours of tuition and 30 hours of evaluated specialist teaching. There is also ATS – Accredited Teacher Status requiring 40 hours of tuition and 20 hours of evaluated specialist teaching. Currently both attributions are only available to teachers and other specific educational professionals. In recognition of the particular needs of post-16 students there are Further and Higher Education variants of these attributions for those working specifically in Colleges and Universities.

Following the same pragmatic philosophy, the significant rise in the number of Support/ Teaching Assistants employed in UK schools has been followed by the creation of the award ALSA – Accredited Learning Support Assistant. These courses are often taught 'in-house' by Local Authorities in liaison with a local Institute of Higher Education. They can, therefore, be readily tailored to the needs of local schools. The two most recent developments are criteria for recognition of teachers with specialist training in mathematics and for those in initial teacher training ATS (ITT). It is hoped to encourage uptake of this opportunity by ITT providers as a vehicle for ensuring that there is a dyslexia specialist in every primary school in the UK. 'Blue-skies' thinking might suggest hope that the requirements for this award become embodied in the general ITT Primary Curriculum. If so, eventually all teachers would become knowledgeable about dyslexia and how to handle it.

The value of such recognition has spread beyond the UK and

there are 'Overseas' variants of accreditations for teachers with non-UK teaching qualifications.

The Board carries out this main function by appointing two of its members as a liaison team to a course wishing to be 'accredited'. Their role is not to dictate detailed content and structure but to ensure that the broad criteria of length of tuition and evaluated teaching, academic standard, level of assessment and quality control are met. They also compare the content of teaching sessions against the outcome criteria agreed by the Board in relation to the award requested. Accreditation is for a four year period but the liaison team remains as a source of support during that period. Should the course team wish to make changes to the content or structure of the course their first approach should be to the liaison team. If good contact has been kept during the four years the reaccreditation should be merely a matter of demonstrating how the course has remained abreast of developments in theory and practice.

Currently there are 25 courses for teachers and lecturers of which four are specifically designed for those working in Further and Higher Education. There are 12 courses for Teaching Assistants, two designated for work in 'Mainstream' schools and one integrated into the final two years of a BA (Hons) Initial Teacher Training course giving both Qualified Teacher Status from the General Teaching Council and Accredited Teachers Status from the BDA.

There are 2,210 individual holders of AMBDA, 247 with AMBDA FE/HE, 1092 with ATS and 114 with ATS FE/HE. Six hundred and eighty six Teaching Assistants have ALSA status. In common with other professions, from January 2009 holders of BDA awards have had to submit details of their professional development activities over the past four years if they wish to remain on the 'Active' register. To date 68 people have done so.

The majority of the holders of AMBDA or ATS have taken one of the courses accredited by the BDA. However, it is possible to apply 'by Individual Merit' (IM). This is not granted lightly, and an application must be based on sound and valid evidence not only of extended successful practice but also of fulfilment of the theoretical criteria contained in accredited courses.

The health of the BDA's work in this area is evidenced by the number of applications received over the past year:

Type of Accreditation	May 2008	September 2008	January 2009	May 2009	Total
AMBDA	51	74	37	33	195
AMBDA FE/HE	14	19	1	12	46
ATS	31	30	10	9	80
ATS FE/HE	7	6	2	2	17
ALSA	57	42	19	33	151
Individual Merit	4	2	3	31	40
Total	164	173	72	120	529

Clearly there is no shortage of people who recognise the need to be appropriately and effectively trained to teach and support learners with dyslexia of all ages. One interesting statistic is the increase in applications for Individual Merit in May 2009 following the introduction of the requirement for continuing professional development. A significant number of these new applications were from people taking the opportunity to request 'upgrading' from ATS to AMBDA as a result of their learning and experience since their initial training course.

The Board is also recognised widely as a source of expertise. For example, one of our members sat on the committee developing the National Literacy and Numeracy Strategy. As part of the development of the Multi-Sensory Teaching System for Reading, every primary school in the country received two copies of the 'Handy Hints' poster for recognising dyslexia. The Qualifications and Curriculum Authority commissioned a report on the readability of A-level and GCSE papers. Through PATOSS it has been influential in developing the requirements for assessors under the Special Educational Needs and Disability Act. Latterly it has been closely involved in presenting evidence to the committee chaired by Jim Rose into the teaching of reading.

On a day-to-day basis members are available to the permanent staff of the BDA to advise on the myriad of dyslexia related questions directed at them! It may not be too strong to say that the Board is at the heart of the BDA's core commitment to early identification and support for those with dyslexia. All children attend schools. Many also attend pre-school provision of one sort or another. The more people there are in such situations who are knowledgeable about dyslexia, its manifestations and effective approaches to its amelioration, the greater the chance that dyslexia will no longer be a barrier to attainment of potential.

Mike Johnson is a member of the BDA Accreditation board

Report from the Local Associations Board

Jeff Hughes

The British Dyslexia Association (BDA) has a network of Local Dyslexia Associations (LDAs) throughout the country. Their activities are many and varied including giving information about dyslexia, advising families, schools, employers and adults on how to deal with dyslexia, holding meetings and events, and campaigning locally to improve understanding and provision. Within the BDA, Local Associations are represented by the Local Associations Board (LAB) which meets four times each year with members of the Trustees and Judi Stewart, our CEO. Issues which affect Local Associations are raised by BDA staff, by Trustees, by Local Dyslexia Associations and by LAB members.

In the recent past the LAB has been concerned to reverse the decline in the number of active LDAs. We are pleased that a number of support groups have been set up and are now to become LDAs. Work is planned to establish new groups in areas without an Association, often starting under the wing of a neighbouring LDA.

To be better able to respond to some regional invitations, the LAB representation has recently been reorganised to coincide with the Government Office Regions. The newly elected representatives take up their posts in June 2009 and over the next three years will take the LAB's work forward. In all areas we will need to find 'Deputy' representatives, and we are hoping to find representatives who are Adult Dyslexics to work with, and to complement, the influential Young Dyslexics representatives.

In the past few years LAB has relied on the support of the LAB members and their Local Association to meet its minimal costs. In particular Jack Haymer, who has been Chair of LAB through an extremely turbulent time, has provided enthusiastic and resourceful leadership. As one of the LAB's representative Trustees Jack has, with Trevor Hobbs and Chris Hossack, provided a direct and influential link with the Management Board of the BDA. This is an important means by which Local Association issues can be raised and dealt with centrally.

Jack and other members of the LAB have been central to organising an annual Family Day at which the BDA meets with its individual members in a relaxed and interesting event. The involvement of one of the young LAB members in organising this year's event suggests that our future activities will be many and successful.

A new LAB meets in July so it is time to thank members who have served their two terms with such dedication and wisdom. Jack Haymer, Trevor Hobbs, Joan Flanneray, Hugh Payton, David Watson and John Clarke will be missed but will no doubt continue to be active in supporting the development of the BDA.

Jeff Hughes is Vice Chair of the LAB.

Report from the New Technologies Committee

Di Hillage

The members of the committee have been involved in a variety of activities as usual during the last year.

In November 2008, at the suggestion of Dr Chris Singleton, we were invited to speak to Sir Jim Rose's Dyslexia Expert Advisory Group which has been reviewing effective ways of supporting pupils with specific learning difficulties in schools. We gave presentations outlining the ways in which technology could be used to support reading and writing, maths, organisation and learning, and to ensure that schools become dyslexia friendly.

Jean Hutchins has been a member, and the driving force behind, the committee since 1985. We were all delighted to hear that her determination and energy in raising awareness of the ways in which technology can support dyslexic people was, at last, rewarded as she was a finalist in the 2008 Access-IT awards.

The stands at BETT and the Education show (see figure 1) were organised once again by Jean with her customary efficiency. Committee members were ably supported on the stands by volunteers from Local Associations. The 2009 BETT seminars were given by EA Draffan and Victoria Crivelli. Both were well received by appreciative audiences. Information in paper and DVD formats was handed out at each event. Seminars at the Education show were given by Dr Kate Saunders and Victoria Crivelli.

EA Draffan, Ian Litterick and Jean contributed to the BDA

Figure 1

International conference in Harrogate. Victoria repeated her presentation as part of the BDA conference in Oxford where she was also a member of one of the expert panels.

Aside from these public events, a good deal of background work by committee members has gone into such activities as...

- writing articles for the Contact magazine and elsewhere, ably coordinated and edited by Cheryl Dobbs
- revising the I.C.T. information published on the BDA website
- supporting local groups directly and by responding to email enquiries
- speaking at various local events around the country and, in some cases, at international events
- making suggestions for updating Accreditation Board criteria and Accessibility Policy for publications, including ensuring

that our material conforms to the latter
- reviewing software and giving feedback to authors
- recommending products for inclusion in the BDA store

Despite all these efforts, we are still brought down to earth from time to time by meeting those involved with dyslexic people, especially in schools, who are still largely unaware of the benefits technology has to offer. The Dyslexia Friendly Schools I.C.T. document, which can be found on the BDA website and which was originally produced by Victoria, obviously still needs to be promoted. We all look forward to continuing our efforts to help dyslexic people make effective use of the technology available to them.

Di Hillage is Chairman of the BDA New Technologies Committee

Reports from the dyslexia organisations

British Dyslexia Association

Judi Stewart

The vision of the British Dyslexia Association (BDA) is a dyslexia-friendly society that enables all dyslexic people to reach their full potential.

The BDA is a membership organisation that provides impartial support, guidance and direction to policy-makers at national and regional level, as well as to parents, children, young people, employers and employees. The BDA is a dynamic charity which raises awareness and provides support and information to people in the UK and around the world.

Our strategic objectives are to:

- work for long lasting and sustainable change for the benefit of dyslexic people
- provide impartial and objective advice and support to dyslexic people and those with whom they come into contact
- set the standards for dyslexia knowledge and professional expertise
- deliver innovative solutions which break new ground in the field of dyslexia
- disseminate and share best practice regionally, nationally and internationally
- promote research.

How the BDA works

The BDA works on a number of levels. The Trustees and Senior Management Team shape and influence policy at the very highest level to ensure that it is well founded and sustainable.

The BDA also advises and supports at a local level through the National Helpline, its national network of local associations, its website and regionally-based projects.

Across each of these levels, the BDA enables people with dyslexia to access appropriate support in school, further education and the workplace; it works to reduce the numbers of dyslexic people entering the criminal justice system and it supports those who are already in it; it assists employers to embrace the potential that dyslexic people offer, and it supports parents and carers with clear, evidence-based information and advice.

In return, information that the BDA receives from 'the ground' highlights gaps and problems in dyslexia support, as well as examples of best practice. From these, new methods, ideas and strategies can develop and become the basis of future change.

Policy

The BDA works strategically with other national and local organisations and government bodies to influence policy decisions for the well-being of dyslexic individuals, their families and employers.

Examples of our policy work include:

- Working as part of the *Dyslexia-SpLD Trust* to support the implementation of the findings of the *Rose Review* (2009), including promoting the training of 4,000 more specialist dyslexia teachers.
- Participating in Disabilities representation with the *National Offenders Management Service*.
- Providing discussion papers and information for the

government (e.g. on *Learning Support for Young Offenders on Community Based Sentences*).

■ Providing input on the needs of dyslexic individuals for the *Joint Council for Qualifications* (JCQ) concerning access arrangements for examinations.

■ Providing input for *Ofqual*, the new regulator of qualifications, exams and tests in England.

■ Working with the *Right to Read* campaign which presses for the publication of the same book, at the same time and at the same price for all print-impaired children and adults, and for publications to be in alternative formats.

■ Working in partnership with the government's *Accessible Resources Pilot Group* to assess accessible resources in schools.

Training

The BDA training provision delivers courses nationwide for teachers, parents and employers. These courses focus on increasing understanding about dyslexia, screening for dyslexia, and making reasonable adjustments for dyslexia. Our courses are built around the most recent research to help a range of audiences to understand the particular needs of dyslexic people, and they offer practical solutions as to how these individuals can best be supported in education and in the workplace.

We offer three types of training:

■ *open courses*, which are practical events for educators and employers;

■ *bespoke courses*, which are tailored to meet the particular needs of schools, colleges or organisations, and are run on their site;

■ and we have two *accredited programmes*, one on dyslexia
and screening, and one on the range of hidden difficulties
(dyslexia, dyscalculia, ADHD, Asperger's and autism) and
how to teach children with these.

We have also recently launched our Work Based Assessors
Programme. This is a programme of accreditation for work
based assessors who offer assessments to individuals with
dyslexia or other the Specific Learning Difficulties to help them
to be aware of the most recent research and applications in this
area[1].

Over the last 12 months we have trained over 3,000 people
and have received many repeat requests for bespoke training.
Whatever the motivation for training, the common reaction is
that dyslexia and related difficulties are more widespread than
envisaged, and our clients display a willingness to instigate
changes to help dyslexic people. As a result we are finding that
the BDA training programmes have considerable effect on the
perception of dyslexia, on understanding of how common it is,
and what can be done to support people with dyslexia in
schools, colleges and at work.

Quality Mark

To support the BDA's vision of a dyslexia-friendly society, we
have continued to expand our Quality Mark scheme. The
Quality Mark is a 'kite mark', which provides recognition that
an organisation is dyslexia-friendly. To demonstrate this, the
whole organisation works through a process of self-assessment
against BDA criteria, development to meet these criteria, and
verification. Schools, local authorities, children's services,
colleges, vocational, educational and training establishments,

1 Full details of all of these courses are available on the BDA website; see also the chapter by
Margaret Malpas in this handbook

universities and employers can achieve the Quality Mark. Dr Kate Saunders has reviewed current developments for the BDA Quality Mark in her chapter in this handbook.

Helpline

The accredited BDA Helpline is run by 25 volunteers and is linked to Local Associations, many of which provide a localised service. The Helpline receives over 1,500 calls a month and 300 emails. Advice, support and information are given for various learning difficulties, not just dyslexia. The web site is an excellent source of information that is regularly updated by Helpline staff, and it receives approximately 27,000 unique hits per month.

Local Association Board

The Local Association Board (LAB) acts as the principal forum of debate concerning Local Dyslexia Association matters including ideas and concerns covering all ages and all aspects of dyslexia in education, employment and the community. The LAB consists of one representative elected from among the Local Associations in each region and it reports directly to the Management Board (Trustee body).

Accreditation Board

In educational terms, the Accreditation Board oversees the 'gold standard' in teacher training internationally. The government has recently committed to fund 4,000 additional teachers to train on BDA accredited courses at Associate Member of the British Dyslexia Association (AMBDA) level and Approved Teacher Status (ATS) level.

The main responsibilities of the BDA Accreditation Board are to:

- approve courses of study
- work with academic institutions to develop new courses
- award individual qualifications to those who successfully complete approved courses
- set standards and criteria for the award of each qualification

Advisory Groups

There are two specialist Advisory Groups which provide the Trustees with expert information as well as assisting the BDA with its work:

- *The New Technologies Committee* works to raise awareness of information and communication technologies (ICT) that may be of use to people with dyslexia in education and the workplace[2]. Committee members publish expert reviews, they provide information and advice, and they regularly give talks and run workshops on the potential of ICT in helping to overcome challenges faced by people with dyslexia.
- *The Music Committee* supports the BDA Helpline by offering advice for music students and professionals on all aspects of music and dyslexia[3]. Members of the committee have written guidelines outlining special arrangements for dyslexic candidates taking the Associated Board of the Royal Schools of Music exams, and they have produced the Music and Dyslexia information sheet on the BDA website.

Membership

During 2009, BDA membership continued to grow. The BDA has been considering making changes to the Local Dyslexia

2 See Di Hillage's report from the New Technologies Committee in this handbook
3 Sheila Oglethorpe, the Chair of the BDA's Music committee has also written a chapter in this handbook

Associations (LDAs) and Dyslexia Support Groups (DSGs) over the past year, and at the AGM held in November 2008 the Membership voted in favour of combining LDAs and DSGs into one membership group.

Projects

The BDA is currently running several projects including:

- *The EQUIPPED (Enabling Quality Information Promoting Positive Education Dyslexia)* Project in Northern Ireland which is funded by the Big Lottery Fund. This is a community-based project which is raising awareness of the complex nature of the learning differences presented by dyslexia, and the importance of early identification if those affected by it are to access much needed support.
- *The Liverpool Dyslexia Project*, funded by the Liverpool Children's Fund, which provides dyslexia awareness training and promotes best practice in dyslexia support for children's services. Fourteen departments of Liverpool's Children's Services achieved the Dyslexia Friendly Quality Mark in Spring 2009.
- The BDA is working in partnership with other organisations under the *Transform Project* which supports offenders and ex offenders into education, training and employment across the Midlands region.
- The BDA has also recently been awarded European Union funding for a two year project called *Dyslexia Veto*. In this project, individuals from the UK and four other European countries (Italy, Hungary, Bulgaria and Romania) will work together to support vocational, educational and training establishments through the Dyslexia Friendly Quality Mark.

The future

The coming year promises to be an exciting one for the BDA. In addition to various new research, training and educational initiatives, we will continue to create change, set standards, and deliver a first-class service to support and enable all people with dyslexia in the UK. We will continue to listen to their views, represents their agendas and press for long lasting sustainable change to meet their needs and improve their lives.

For further information about any aspect of the BDA's work, please contact:

The British Dyslexia Association,
Unit 8, Bracknell Beeches
Old Bracknell Lane
Bracknell,
RG12 7BW.

Tel (Helpline): 0845 251 9002
Tel (Admin): 0845 251 9003
Fax: 0845 251 9005
Web: www.bdadyslexia.org.uk

Judi Stewart is Chief Executive of the British Dyslexia Association

The dyslexia friendly-user friendly campaign: creating a more inclusive society for dyslexics

Donald Schloss

The Adult Dyslexia Organisation (ADO) is a national body run by dyslexics for dyslexics and all those concerned with adult dyslexics. We promote the cause of adults with dyslexia through lobbying, research, training and campaigning, and in the design and delivery of services. Donald Schloss, the chief executive and campaign leader, is himself severely dyslexic. He has led ADO in raising awareness of the needs of dyslexics in prisons, employment and education. Donald and the ADO have won many awards for their services, and have significant contacts and active participation nationally and worldwide.

Launched in May 2005, the *Dyslexia Friendly – User Friendly* campaign has benefited not just dyslexics but everybody, increasing awareness about dyslexia and campaigning for accessibility so people with dyslexia can reach their full potential.

The campaign creates awareness and benefits:

- In education, about dyslexics' need for support for their different way of learning
- Among employers, employees, managers and trade unions regarding reasonable adjustments to maximize the productivity of dyslexics

- About assistive technology on policy and content of websites, meeting the needs of dyslexics for accessibility, e.g. through the Readback facility
- Through support groups, sponsorship, specialist dyslexia support, and donations
- Through adjustments within public services to improve the day-to-day living of dyslexics
- Through guides and downloadable guidelines from www.adult-dyslexia.org
- Through innovative training courses that are face to face and online

What is Dyslexia?

Challenging the negative view of dyslexia as a *disability, we* believe that it is an experience arising from natural human diversity, and not a 'deficit' incorrectly linked to intelligence. In practical terms, it is disabling to expect that everyone thinks, learns, reads, takes notes, and takes in multiple instructions in the same way. Let's turn this around. If we expect everyone to think fluently in 3D, as most dyslexics can, the majority of the population might be considered disabled.

We prefer to promote attitudes and strategies that are more inclusive and less likely to disable anyone – hence the slogan: Dyslexia-Friendly, User-Friendly.

In negative environments dyslexics are indeed disabled, and therefore entitled to support – the Disabled Students' Allowance, and for employees the protection of the Disability Discrimination Act.

Why sign up to the Campaign?

It can cost little, but gives benefits:

- **Workplace**. Outcomes can improve productivity
- **Education**. Increases retention and course completion
- **ICT**. Gives guidance on building more accessible websites
- **Daily Living**. Helps individuals reach their full potential within the community

Groups can share coping strategies to build self esteem and reach their full potential through user-led ownership. You can support awareness-raising by taking part in training, poster campaigns, newsletters, and media events, or signing up to the campaign commitments.

Join the campaign for a more inclusive society!

The Adult Dyslexia Organisation, Ground Floor,
Secker House, Minet Road,
Loughborough Estate, London, SW9 7TP.
Tel: 020 7207 3911

Email: ado.dns@dial.pipex.com
Website: www.adult-dyslexia.org

Donald Schloss is Chief Executive of the Adult Dyslexia Organisation

Arts Dyslexia Trust

Susan Parkinson

The year has been one of continuing consolidation of reorganisation after the Trust's change of premises, and the very sad loss of our President, Malcolm Ritchie, who died a few months ago. Malcolm was a founding member of ADT and an important influence on all the Trust's policy decisions. We miss him greatly.

However, we are delighted that Malcolm's son, Rupert, has taken over as President. In many ways Rupert is following in Malcolm's footsteps. He shares his father's passion for the theatre and studied at the Central School of Speech & Drama where he took his B.Ed degree in 1996. He has since gathered wide experience of teaching. He qualified as a specialist teacher of dyslexic children and adults in 1989 and has qualifications in the Rudolf Steiner system and the Alexander Technique. He has conducted many workshops for the English Touring Theatre, LTTC London, the Rose Theatre, amongst others, and most recently the National Theatre. He is now a LAMDA examiner/teacher.

Though not officially assessed as dyslexic himself, as an ex-pupil of Brickwall House, Rupert has many dyslexic friends and is very familiar with both the difficulties they face and their often unrecognised talents.

Many new members have joined us this year, among them: Denis Argent, who is now the Trustee responsible for overseeing the ADT's financial affairs; Catherine Black who is researching visual-spatial ability and its connection with dyslexia; film-maker Cecilia Frugiuele; and ground-breaking artist Sandra Zaman.

One of the highlights of the year was the ADT social afternoon, at which bright young members together with the older hands showed their work and exchanged views. The atmosphere buzzed with exciting ideas. Jonathan Adams, Stephen Garrett, Joc Marchington, Stephen Gaull talked about their recent and forthcoming exhibitions. Catherine Black presented her filmed "Rotation" tests, sparking much discussion. Geoff Ball told us about his survey of moths in Nottinghamshire where unusual specimens were discovered, his project combining sculpture and electro-dynamics, and his recent exhibitions featuring a series of paintings based on his vast experience of geology.

A big London exhibition is being planned by ADT for 2010 which will also tour Universities and Colleges throughout Britain. The aim is to spread greater understanding of visual-spatial creative talent, as often displayed by dyslexics.

We have many other projects which space does not allow me to detail. And there are many members whose stalwart support and valuable work we would mention here if space permitted. Danni Knight for one, has contributed unbelievable amounts of time and energy to our endeavours.

For the rest, it has been a hard slog writing out applications for sponsorship. Not a job any of us is good at (!) but I expect that has been a similar story for other groups. Nevertheless, we continue to live in hope!

As always our helpline has been busy. Please, if you would like to take part in any ADT projects, ring us: 01233 811960 (pm.)

Susan Parkinson is CEO of the Arts Dyslexia Trust

Bangor Dyslexia Unit

Marie Jones

The Dyslexia Unit at Bangor University has had a year of both highs and lows. The loss of Professor Tim Miles OBE who, with his wife Elaine, established the Unit in the mid 60s was a devastating blow. His work in the field of dyslexia was pioneering and he remained actively involved in that work up to his death in December 2008. He will be greatly missed by his many friends and colleagues. The annual TR Miles lecture given by Professor Dorothy Bishop on May 21st, and a Dyslexia Unit conference on October 24th, celebrated his work.

Appointment of Director

At the start of the academic year we were delighted that Dr Marketa Caravolas was appointed as new Director of the Unit and Senior Lecturer in the School of Psychology. Dr Caravolas' work focuses on how various aspects of language develop and interact with the cognitive processes underlying early literacy development. She is currently leading the Marie Curie funded project ELDEL (Enhancing Literacy Development in European Languages).

Services

The Unit continues to provide a range of services to support dyslexic children and adults, and specialises in assessment, teaching and training. The Student Service supports university students through individual and group sessions following initial screening or assessment. The Assessment Service offers full psychological assessment of children and adults, and the

Q. What do we need when we are learning to read?

A. Simple vocabulary at the start.

A clear logical progression of phonics.

Appealling illustrations and uncluttered pages.

The 110 Jelly and Bean books provide all these

and more ....

www.jellyandbean.co.uk

Jelly and Bean Ltd. Unit 4A   Follifoot Ridge Business Park
Pannal Road Harrogate HG3 1DP
Tel: 01423 879182   Fax: 01423 874307
email: jellyandbean@mac.com

Teaching Service provides individual and group teaching support in local schools, through its specialist team, following referral from three LEAs. The Teaching Service also provides teaching support privately on request. Part-time courses on dyslexia for qualified teachers are run through the Bangor University School of Education and Lifelong Learning Master's Programme.

New Developments

Dyslexic students registered with the Student Service are participating in an 'Involving Students' project, while the Student Service has joined the Assessment Service in the formation of HEARTS (Higher Education and Reporting Team). The Student Service has also developed a new training module entitled 'Working with Dyslexia'. This provides training for Mentors/Learning Coaches working with the 14-19 years age group, and spans the transition between school and work.

The Teaching Service has set up a new bilingual dyslexia course for Learning Support Assistants (ALSA). The Bangor Dyslexia Unit Certificate Course for LSAs: Supporting Learners with Specific Learning Difficulties (Dyslexia) is validated through the College of Education and Lifelong Learning at Bangor University for 20 credits at Level 4/Undergraduate Level 1, and accredited through the BDA.

Teaching Resources

Specialist teachers at the Unit continue to be at the forefront in the development of new and updated dyslexia teaching resources available in Welsh. Following the success of the set of reading books 'Pitrwm Patrwm', a further set of books for older children is underway, and a set for younger children is in the planning stages. We are also pleased to announce that the revision of the Welsh teaching programme 'O Gam I Gam' has been completed.

To find out more visit our website:
www.dyslexia.bangor.ac.uk

Marie Jones is Director of Teaching at Bangor Dyslexia Unit

Council for the Registration of Schools Teaching Dyslexic Pupils

Brendan Wignall

CReSTeD was established in 1989 to help parents in the difficult task of choosing a school for their children with dyslexia. Many schools claim to offer help for dyslexic pupils but it can be difficult to know which schools actually deliver good provision. By providing a listing of schools that have been visited and approved for their provision, the CReSTeD accreditation process can give parents confidence when drawing up a shortlist. Once approved, schools are re-visited every three years to ensure that their standards are maintained. Information on schools is published on the CReSTeD website and in an annually printed 'Register of Schools' which is distributed free of charge to parents and other interested people.

It has been a busy year for CReSTeD. The decision was taken to include other specific learning difficulties such as dyspraxia and dyscalculia in the accreditation process, and to pass on this information to parents via the website and Register. There has been the opportunity to contribute to the Rose Review on dyslexia and also to the work of the recently formed All Party Parliamentary Group on Dyslexia and Specific Learning Difficulties.

CReSTeD continues to work actively in co-operation with other dyslexia bodies, most notably the British Dyslexia Association and Dyslexia Action, both of which have representatives on the CReSTeD Council. A particular feature of this co-operation has been the pilot project to develop a new category of schools specifically relevant to maintained sector schools offering provision for dyslexia. This follows on from the excellent work that has been done over a number of years through the collaboration between Portsmouth Education Authority and Dyslexia Action.

No two pupils with SpLD are the same or have the same requirements. CReSTeD has thereforeDivided the list of schools into categories according to their provision, ranging from Specialist Provision for those needing a high level of support, to Withdrawal System for those needing just a little extra help each week. The Register also includes a checklist of things to look for and questions to ask when visiting a school; these have proved very helpful to parents.

For more information on CReSTeD and the Register of Schools, please visit the website www.crested.org.uk or contact the Administrator on 01242 604852.

Brendan Wignall is the Chair of CReSTeD

Dyslexia Action

Kerry Bennett

Dyslexia Action is a national educational charity and the UK's leading provider of services and support for people with dyslexia and literacy difficulties. We specialise in assessments, teaching and training as well as developing and distributing teaching materials and undertaking research.

Dyslexia Action improves lives through education. Our mission is to ensure that all individuals with dyslexia are identified and appropriately supported. We do this by:

- providing screening and assessment
- providing specialist teaching
- developing specialist teaching and support materials
- working to influence and improve the practice of mainstream educational services for children and adults with dyslexia
- evaluating teaching methods to achieve better practice improving awareness and understanding of dyslexia

Each year we provide diagnostic assessments for over 9,000 children and adults, teach over 4,000 children and adults, and train over 200 teachers on our postgraduate courses. As well as providing specialist tuition for literacy, most of our teaching centres run study skills courses and offer tuition in numeracy. We provide specialist training courses for teachers, parents and others who are interested in dyslexia and literacy. Our postgraduate attendance courses are held around the UK and are also available to teachers throughout the world by distance learning. Shorter, specialist courses for teachers, teaching assistants, adult tutors and parents are offered at a range of UK centres, as well as tailor-made courses to suit individual need.

Additional services and partnerships include:

1. Consultancy with employers

Dyslexia Action works with companies to advise on the best options for them and their employees to support work performance in line with the DDA. This includes work-focused psychological assessment followed by a workplace consultation for individuals or groups.

2. Consultancy with schools and other providers

We work with schools, colleges, universities and private trainers to address the needs of their students; sometimes our teachers work directly with learners, or alongside SENCOs and/or teaching assistants.

Our whole school intervention programme, Partnership for Literacy, where we have partnered with 35 primary schools since January 2006, has been very successful. The evaluations have shown positive outcomes in terms of gains made by the children involved but also in terms of giving schools the resources and training that they can then embed into their teaching practices.

3. Contract services

This includes partnerships with organisations such as the Learning and Skills Council or Jobcentre Plus to provide screening, awareness training, assessment and tuition targeted to specific groups of people such as those living in deprived areas, or those working in key industries.

We also work with other agencies and charities to promote or develop services, for example, with parents or local communities.

4. Probation, prison and young offender services

We offer a range of services that have proved invaluable to probation, prison and young offenders groups. This also contributes to our ongoing research.

Contact us:

Dyslexia Action
Park House, Wick Road, Egham, Surrey, TW20 0HH
T: 01784 222300 F: 01784 222333
E: info@dyslexiaaction.org.uk
W: www.dyslexiaaction.org.uk

Kerry Bennett is Communications & Policy Manager at Dyslexia Action

The Dyslexia Association of Ireland

Rosie Bissett

The Dyslexia Association of Ireland (DAI) was founded in 1972. It is a company, limited by guarantee, and a voluntary organisation with charitable status. It aims to promote awareness of dyslexia/Specific Learning Difficulty (SpLD) and to serve the needs of people with this difficulty.

The Association currently has 31 branches which act as parent support groups in local areas, provide information, and run out-of-school facilities (workshops) for children. The association also provides services for adults with dyslexia/SpLD. Membership of the Association is open to anyone concerned with promoting the treatment and prevention of the problems associated with dyslexia/SpLD. The Association represents almost 2,700 families all over Ireland. Its membership also includes teachers and psychologists.

The DAI is a founder member of the European Dyslexia Association which now has over 25 member countries; it is a founder member of Spectrum, an umbrella group for people with hidden learning disabilities; a corporate member of the BDA; a member of the Disability Federation of Ireland (DFI), and the National Adult Literacy Agency (NALA).

What does the Association do?

The Association lobbies for the provision of appropriate services by the state to all people with dyslexia, and it is actively involved in fundraising to enable the provision of subsidised services to those individuals and families facing financial disadvantage. It also provides:

- A free information service to the public – post, telephone, email, website and a drop-in service at our Dublin office
- Psycho-educational assessment of children and adults. The Association accepts referrals from parents, teachers, doctors and psychologists, and will arrange testing for anyone with queried dyslexia
- Group and individual tuition to children and adults. Specialised help is offered to pupils aged 7-18 in centres around the country
- A countrywide list of specialist teachers/tutors who give private one-to-one tuition to people with dyslexia. This list is only available to our members
- Non-residential summer schools each July offering language and mathematical tuition
- An innovative full-time course for unemployed adults with dyslexia (administered by FÁS)
- In-service courses for qualified teachers on many aspects of dyslexia/SpLD
- Speakers to school and parent groups on how to help and support dyslexic children
- Dyslexia awareness training for companies, on request
- Training and support to our network of branches and workshops nationwide to ensure best practice
- Seminars on relevant topics
- An Annual Conference and AGM each year in April, and a major European conference once every three years

Information and literature is available from the national office. DAI has various publications including "All Children Learn Differently: A Parents' Guide to Dyslexia" and "Dyslexia: An Irish Perspective". A new book for adults on dyslexia – "Living with Dyslexia" – has recently been launched (along with an audio CD version).

Contact:

Dyslexia Association of Ireland, Suffolk Chambers, 1 Suffolk Street, Dublin 2.

Tel: 01 6790276
Fax: 01 6790273
Website: www.dyslexia.ie
Email: info@dyslexia.ie

Rosie Bissett is Director of the Dyslexia Association of Ireland

Dyslexia Scotland

Cathy Magee

Dyslexia Scotland is both a registered charity (SCO00951) and a company limited by guarantee (No. SC 153321). Based in Stirling with branches run by volunteers, Dyslexia Scotland represents the needs and interests of dyslexic people in Scotland.

Our services include:

- National Telephone Helpline, Monday – Friday, 10am – 4pm
- National tutor list and training for tutors
- Supporting Projects in partnership with key partners including Universities, the Scottish Government, Branches:
- Count Me In; Dyslexia at Transition; Supporting Dyslexic Pupils in the Secondary Curriculum
- Website, leaflets and guides
- Adult Network with quarterly meetings
- Conferences, Workshops and Training events
- Quarterly Magazine and a variety of services for members
- A range of local services provided through the 12 local branches
- A national voice (influencing policy)
- National Mentoring Scheme (in partnership with the BDA and Cass Business School)

In 2008/09, there have been a number of significant positive developments in Scotland in relation to dyslexia:

- At the Dyslexia Summit in January 2008, a groundbreaking

commitment was made to develop a two year action plan,
Framework for Inclusion, to identify professional
knowledge, understanding, skills and values required by
teachers throughout their careers. *Framework for Inclusion*
launched in April 2009

■ Adoption of a working definition on dyslexia by the Scottish
Government, Dyslexia Scotland and the Cross Party Group
on Dyslexia in January 2009

■ In October 2008, Her Majesty's Inspectorate for Education
(HMIE) published a milestone report **'Education for
learners with dyslexia'.** This evidenced examples of
outstanding practice, and identified that there was
considerable scope for development to maximise the
potential of every learner with dyslexia

■ In January 2009, Dyslexia Scotland established a Dyslexia
Assessments Working Group to develop a web-based
resource for use by teachers for the assessment of dyslexia.
Supported by the Scottish Government, this will enable
teachers to plan appropriate support for dyslexic
learners. Account will be taken of the recommendations in
the above HMIE review, and assessment will be based on
the agreed working definition of dyslexia

Governance, staff and volunteer developments

In October 2008, following consultation with its members,
Dyslexia Scotland made significant changes to its structure and
governance. The Board of Directors is now the governing
body, advised by its Members Representative Council, made
up of Branch representatives.

The same consultation process informed Dyslexia Scotland's Strategic Plan which is now in place for the next 3 years (2009 – 2012). This will be delivered through six sub groups and monitored by the Board of Directors.

In August 2008, a National Development Officer was appointed to support existing and potential branches across Scotland. Funded by the Eranda Foundation, this post has been extended to 2012. Two new Branches have been established, Dyslexia Scotland Hebrides in Lewis and Dyslexia Scotland West Lothian.

For further details contact:
Dyslexia Scotland, Stirling Business Centre, Wellgreen, Stirling, FK8 2DZ.

Email: info@dyslexiascotland.org.uk
Website: www.dyslexiascotland.org.uk
Telephone: 01786 44 66 50

Dyslexia Scotland Helpline: 0844 800 84 84

Cathy Magee is Chief Executive of Dyslexia Scotland

Dyslexia Wales

Caroline Keen

The Dyslexia Wales workshops are a hands-on, fun, creative experience which rely on the commitment and participation of both parties to develop a successful working partnership. Each client is guided through six days of one-to-one workshops which go to the root cause of dyslexia and any associated conditions such as:

- Dyspraxia
- Dysphasia
- Dyscalculia
- Bedwetting
- Hyperactivity
- Attention Deficit Disorder
- Specific Learning Difficulties

The Dyslexia Wales workshops aim to remove learning blocks and empower clients to take personal responsibility for their learning. They do not rely on costly drugs, machinery or appliances.

Dyslexia Wales engages each client in a process of discovery to identify his or her goals, strengths and weaknesses. The client is then guided through a course of workshops tailored to meet his or her individual needs. No two courses are the same. Each course is designed to release the individual's full potential, and clients are frequently overjoyed by the result.

A home follow-up programme is designed during which the client practises the techniques learnt, then a development day to review and support progress is arranged some weeks later.

People with dyslexia gain self-esteem and confidence once they can access their natural abilities. Progress is very rapid once they discover study methods which capitalise on their talents.

Satisfaction is guaranteed on a Dyslexia Wales course. If a client does not make progress the full cost of the course is cheerfully refunded. Many references are available, as are opportunities to speak to past clients about their experience of the Dyslexia Wales approach.

For more information and to book a **free assessment** contact:

DYSLEXIA WALES

Ysgubor Fawr, Talley, Llandeilo, SA19 7YY
Telephone 01558 685 644
Email: info@dyslexiawales.com
www.dyslexiawales.com

Dyslexia Wales is a private practice. We regret that we have no public funding and so are unable to offer subsidised places.

Caroline Keen is founder of Dyslexia Wales, and she now practises privately, helping people with dyslexia and associated conditions on a one-to-one basis

Helen Arkell Dyslexia Centre

Bernadette McLean

Over the last year, the Helen Arkell Dyslexia Centre (HADC) has consolidated its position as one of the leading trainers of Specialist Teachers.

As a result of the increased demand for the HADC Professional Courses, plans are in place to offer additional courses during the 2009/2010 academic year.

In addition to Specialist Teacher Training, the Centre continues to offer subsidised consultations, assessments by a range of trained professionals, and specialist tuition.

Consultations are offered to parents who are concerned about their children, and to adults who are worried about their studies or employment.

Educational Psychologist Assessments are most important for individuals with complex conditions that co-morbidity may nowadays present. We have, over the past year, added three highly talented Educational Psychologists to our team. However, HADC are finding a rapidly increasing demand for Specialist Teacher Assessments for those with less complex problems which tend to be purely literacy based. Our Specialist Teacher Assessments are carried out by a team of trained experts and schools are increasingly asking for their services.

HADC has been funded to carry out research on the transition of pupils from primary to secondary education. The philosophy behind this being that if a pupil has the necessary remedial help at an early stage then transition to the secondary school, where there is a higher expectation of performance but not necessarily the availability of remedial help, will be made considerably easier; this will enable teachers to concentrate on teaching the class as a whole.

HADC is involved in many aspects of the management of dyslexia, and the quality control of relevant qualifications. They are pleased to be a member of the newly formed Dyslexia SpLD Trust which is a consortium of lead players in the world of dyslexia.

Over the past year, our mini conferences have helped to address the credit crunch in offering short and inexpensive conferences on Saturday mornings, one per term; on the last two occasions we were heavily over-subscribed. Delegates are pleased to have Continual Professional Development out of school time but not taking up all of their weekend, and they appreciate the opportunity to hear top quality speakers who seem happy to travel a distance to come to Frensham.

Our summer schools grow in popularity and we maintain our Norwegian connections by offering a summer school to a group of pupils who travel here from Norway. The teachers who work on these summer schools have countless stories of children who come to life and begin to learn, so making their jobs very satisfying.

We don't only work with school-age children; our clients range from pre-school children to Senior Citizens. We are currently offering services and training in a variety of organisations such as the Probation Service, the RAF and the National Childbirth Trust.

Finally, we are all enthusiastic about the "new Look" HADC which will be seen shortly on our new website and logo. Visit www.arkellcentre.org.uk for further details.

Bernadette McLean is Principal of the Helen Arkell Dyslexia Centre

Patoss

Lynn Greenwold

As the Professional Association of Teachers of Students with Specific Learning Difficulties, Patoss is for all those concerned with the teaching and support of pupils with SpLD: dyslexia, dyspraxia, attention deficit disorder, Asperger's syndrome. We aim to promote good practice amongst professionals and have published guidelines for those moving into this field as well as for parents and established practitioners.

Patoss constantly works to improve standards in teaching and assessment, advise government on policies affecting those with SpLD, and build links with others working in the SpLD community.

Patoss offers:

- links with other professionals
- practising certificates to underpin professional standards
- opportunities to keep in touch with recent research, and to exchange knowledge and experience
- a range of publications
- reduced fees for Patoss national conferences and local events
- a growing network of local groups
- different levels of insurance including professional indemnity

Publications

We continue to work closely with the Joint Council for Qualifications in publishing guidelines in assessing for Access

Arrangements in examinations (*Dyslexia: Assessing for Access Arrangements*). In addition *Dyslexia: Assessing and Reporting – The Patoss Guide* focuses on the purposes, principles and practicalities of assessing for dyslexia across successive age groups. These books join our popular *How Dyslexics Learn: Grasping the Nettle*. We also publish a regularly-updated *Tutor Index*.

Membership

Membership is open to professionals training or working in the field of SpLD. Many members teach and assess in schools and colleges; a number also work independently providing diagnostic assessments and one to one tuition. In addition we offer supporting membership to individuals who have an interest in SpLD and wish to support the aims and activities of Patoss.

The SpLD Assessment Practising Certificate

Pressure for effective monitoring of standards in assessment has grown – from bodies such as Local Authorities, the Department for Children, Schools and Families (DCSF), Department for Innovation, Universities and Skills (DIUS) and Awarding Bodies who use assessment reports to make important decisions, and from within the profession itself. This has led to the development of a SpLD Assessment Practising Certificate. These practising certificates recognise professional achievement in skills as an SpLD assessor. They also link the holder's practice to a commitment to continuing professional development. Holders of the Patoss SpLD Assessment Practising Certificates fulfil the criteria established by the government. These Practising Certificates will, additionally, assure Heads of Centres that the professional is suitably qualified to conduct assessments for examination access arrangements.

The Dyslexia-SpLD Trust

Following the completion of the No to Failure campaign, Patoss is proud to chair the new Dyslexia-SpLD Trust which launched in the Spring of 2009. Working with a board drawn from Patoss, the BDA, Dyslexia Action, the Helen Arkell Dyslexia Centre, Springboard for Children, and Xtraordinary People, the Trust will build a strong consortium to drive forward the agenda to ensure better outcomes for pupils with SpLD.

To find out more

Visit the Patoss website: www.patoss-dyslexia.org
The Dyslexia-SpLD Trust website: www.thedyslexia-spldtrust.org.uk

Lynn Greenwold is the CEO of Patoss Ltd

Xtraordinary People

Kate Griggs

Richard Branson speaks openly about his struggles at school and his dyslexia, in Xtraordinary People's new 'talking stories' for kids

2008 saw the No to Failure project well underway and now under the watchful eye of the steering group which has enabled Xtraordinary People to forge ahead with our main objective – raising awareness around the enormous talents that dyslexics have.

In 2009 we've launched a series of downloadable 'talking stories' for kids, featuring famous dyslexics past and present. One story features a moving interview with Sir Richard Branson who talks openly about his struggles at school, and how he was always bottom of the class! He also shares his view on how dyslexia can be an advantage, and attributes it to part of his success which he hopes will encourage children to focus on their strengths.

The other stories feature Thomas Edison and Winston Churchill with more in the pipeline. They can be downloaded from www.xtraordinarypeople/shop

Kate Griggs says "We've developed these stories to give teachers and parents a better understanding of what it's like to be dyslexic, and most importantly, to inspire dyslexic kids to realise that they can achieve great things, to believe in themselves."

"People think dyslexia is just about reading but we know it's much more than that often creating problems with writing, maths, concentration and getting your thoughts on paper – so school work in general. Yet with the right support these children can excel, something I've seen first hand with my own sons who are both dyslexic."

"The stories, told from a child's perspective, give an insight into all the other things we know cause problems for dyslexic kids like being disorganised, not being able to tell the time, or not being able to concentrate."

Dyslexics have huge strengths too – just a different way of thinking. They're creative, big picture thinkers with amazing imaginations, strengths that have helped many dyslexics to shape our modern world – geniuses like Einstein, inventors like Thomas Edison (the electric light bulb), the Wright brothers (airplanes), Alexander Graham Bell (the telephone), and JFK, Winston Churchill, Walt Disney, Steven Spielberg, Richard Branson and Jamie Oliver – who are all thought to be dyslexic.

Xtraordinary People hopes that by highlighting dyslexics' talents, schools and parents will be motivated to identify dyslexic children and support their difficulties and nurture their talents.

Here's what some people have said about the stories:

"These stories are great because it really helped to know that other kids are going through the same thing as me, this makes me feel much better" – Lucy, aged 9

"Now I know I'm not stupid even though I can't read yet"
– Scott, aged 7

"Richard Branson was bad at maths, just like me. Cool"
– Taylor, aged 11

"A great tool to build self-esteem with the dyslexics I support" – Rachel, a teacher

"I wholeheartedly support Xtraordinary People, as like me, they see dyslexia as a gift – just a different approach to viewing the world." – Sir Richard Branson

For further information visit our website
www.xtraordinarypeople.com

Kate Griggs is founder of Xtraordinary People

Recently published books on dyslexia

Brunswick, N. (2009). **Dyslexia. A Beginner's Guide**. Oxford: Oneworld Publications.

Lawrence, D. (2009). **Understanding Dyslexia: A Guide for Teachers and Parents**. Maidenhead: Open University Press

Massey, J. (2008). **Meeting the Needs of Students with Dyslexia**. London: Network Continuum.

Miles, T., Westcombe, J. and Ditchfield, D. (Eds.) (2008). **Music and Dyslexia: A Positive Approach**. Oxford: Wiley-Blackwell.

Moody, S. (Ed.) (2009). **Dyslexia and Employment: A Guide for Assessors, Trainers and Managers**. Oxford: Wiley-Blackwell.

Muter, V. and Likierman, H. (2008). **Dyslexia: A Parents' Guide to Dyslexia, Dyspraxia and Other Learning Difficulties**. London: Vermilion.

Nicolson, R.I. and Fawcett, A. (2008). **Dyslexia, Learning, and the Brain**. Cambridge, MA: MIT Press

Reid, G. (Ed.) (2009). **The Routledge Companion to Dyslexia**. London: Routledge

Reid, G., Fawcett, A., Manis, F. & Siegel, L. (Eds) (2008). **The SAGE Handbook of Dyslexia**. London: Sage Publishers

Riddick; B. (2009). **Living with Dyslexia, 2nd edition**. London: Routledge

Thomson, M. (2009). **The Psychology of Dyslexia: A Handbook for Teachers, 2nd edition**. Oxford: Wiley-Blackwell

Index of Advertisers